S0-DYU-359

Margaret Stringer
Jer. 33:3

JESUS
LED ME ALL THE WAY

40 Years in the Jungles of Papua, Indonesia

MARGARET STRINGER

PRESS

Jesus Led Me All the Way
40 Years in the Jungles of Papua, Indonesia
by Margaret Stringer

Printed in the United States of America

ISBN 9781498403030

Scripture quotations taken from the King James version of the Holy Bible.

www.xulonpress.com

DEDICATION

I would like to dedicate this book to the following people:

1. That highly favored group of people who have been called by God, and commissioned to go as His ambassadors to find the lost and bring them to Himself. They are missionaries. My prayer that this book will encourage them to remain committed to Him remembering that the One who called them will accomplish His purpose through them as they remain faithful.
2. My family whom I love very much.
3. My fellow missionaries in Papua whose unending patience for 40 years is deeply appreciated.
4. The churches and individuals who were so faithful to support me with your financial support, love, and encouragement.
5. Finally, I would also like to dedicate this book to my dear friend and co-worker Gail Vinje, who served with me for about 25 years in Papua. Gail went to Papua in 1977 as a registered nurse and served faithfully for 35 years. She was diagnosed with inoperable pancreatic cancer in 2010, and was forced to come home for medical help. Although she was told that she would probably live only a few months, she lived for three years and graduated to Heaven on July 20, 2013. Gail's response to

cancer impacted hundreds of lives. Her cheerful, trusting attitude inspired all who knew her. She never complained, and never doubted God's perfect love.

She was cheerful and loved to laugh. When something struck her as being especially funny it was hard to turn off her "giggle box." I miss that so much.

Gail, "sampai jumpa"–until we meet.

ACKNOWLEDGMENTS

My grateful thanks to every individual who contributed in helping to make this book a reality.

Grateful Thanks To

Many of my dear friends and supporters who encouraged me to write this book.

My niece, Debbie Stringer, married to my nephew, Doug, who never stopped believing in me, and prayed for me all the way to the completion.

Terry Thacker, who so patiently checked the manuscript and offered very helpful suggestions.

My good friend, Myra Smith, who also very carefully checked the manuscript.

FOREWORD

The opportunity to write the Foreword for this book, written by "MY HERO" Margaret Stringer, is a great privilege and honor. As I pondered why she would ask a simple, little-known church member to write something for her book, I thought, "That is just like her." She could have chosen from any number of well-known pastors, authors, missionaries, and others, but true to her precious character, she doesn't see big "I's and little "you's". Margaret is one of the most humble, down to earth, godly ladies I have ever met and she would never make anyone feel 'beneath' her. She is a true example of "... the ornament of a meek and quiet spirit, which is in the sight of God of great price."

It has been said that it is yet to be seen what could be done with one life that is totally surrendered to God. It is certain that the Lord Jesus is our only perfect example, but I don't know of another Christian who is a more beautiful picture of a surrendered life than Margaret Stringer. She was saved at the early age of twelve, surrendered to be a missionary as a teenager, never married, spent over forty years in the jungles of Indonesia, and is spending her later years encouraging and teaching others how to be led of Jesus. The Bible speaks of Christian lives being epistles read of all men. What an epistle! What a life!

As you read this book, you will get a glimpse into the jungles of Indonesia and the difficult circumstances, adversities, dangers, and harsh conditions that Margaret Stringer endured for over 40 years, for the cause of

Christ. You will also be introduced to some of the individuals whose lives were changed for time and eternity because one young lady surrendered her life to be a missionary in the deepest, darkest jungles of the world.

If a book were written about your life and my life, I wonder how many individuals we could introduce whose lives have been changed? As an older Christian, reading this book makes me wish I had another life to give! I don't have another life, but I'm reminded of the scripture in Philippians 3:14 that says, "... forgetting those things which are behind, and reaching forth unto those things which are before, I press toward the mark for the prize of the high calling of God in Christ Jesus."

One of the wonderful truths about the Word of God is that God includes the faults and failures of the great men and women of the Bible. We sometimes seem to think that they were superhuman and we could not possibly be used of God like them. We read in Acts where Paul and Barnabas said, "... We also are men of like passions with you." In this book, Margaret shares some of her personal feelings and failures hoping to encourage others to understand that when we feel discouraged or when we fail, by the grace of God we too can press on and be greatly used of God.

I have often heard Margaret share her heart's desire to be an encouragement and a help to others, especially to young Christians and young missionaries. My name can be added to the list of those encouraged! Along with my precious friend Margaret Stringer, it is my desire and prayer that, whether young or old, reading this book will encourage you to be led of Jesus all the way!

Myra Smith, Missions Clerk at Morning Star
Baptist Church

INTRODUCTION

In most books of a biographical nature one normally begins at the beginning, "I was born on October 16, 1939......" However, I found it more interesting to begin with the present, and interpret the past from what I know now.

In our early years of life we normally tend to ask a lot of questions. Why is my life like this? Why is this happening to me? Many of those questions are answered or better understood by experiences in our adult lives. With that in mind, and since experiences I had as an adult have made God's dealings with me as a child to be seen more clearly, I will incorporate experiences from my earlier life throughout this book.

Every book, in my opinion, should have a purpose – to inform, to teach, to encourage, or simply to entertain. My desire with this book is to encourage. I hope that missionaries, whether novice or veteran, will be encouraged and challenged by what they read in these pages. I also pray that others will be challenged to remember the privilege that we have to serve the King of Kings. Serving God in full time ministry is exciting, rewarding, and fun – most of the time. There are also times of extreme discouragement, loneliness, sickness, and danger. In this book I will share many of these experiences.

As you read, please keep in mind that the country where I served went through several name changes during the 40 years that I was there. Those names were:

Dutch New Guinea, Irian Barat (West Irian), Irian Jaya, and finally Papua, which is not to be confused with Papua New Guinea, which is the eastern half of the same island and a totally different country.

PREFACE

The following is an article I wrote for the Mission Magazine, HORIZONS, in 1984 entitled "GRUB WORM JELLY ROLLS." I had been on the field 20 years when this was written and continued there for another 20 years before retiring.

GRUB WORM JELLY ROLLS
The Guts of the Gospel

The Citak people with whom I work in Irian Jaya (now Papua) have no word for love. Their closest word to "love" means "to pity". Only 28 percent of the New Testament is translated into their language, and probably less than 2 percent of the tribe can read it. So the vast majority of the Citak people will not understand God's love from reading the Bible. Since they do not understand unconditional love, on either the human or spiritual level, it must be translated for them through our lives.

In translating the New Testament into their language, I must first understand what the Scripture is saying, and then make it say that same thing in Citak. If the Citak people are to understand God's love, then I must first understand His love, and then love them with the same kind of love – in Citak. Jesus loved individuals. He understood their particular needs.

Sometimes we think people of a primitive culture do not have problems and concerns, just because they don't worry about things that cause great concern in our culture. I remember a young Citak girl named Bu. Bu came into our hospital very sick and emaciated. The medical staff could not find any real disease, but it was obvious Bu was about to die. She violently refused to take any medicine or to eat any food. We were tempted to lose patience with her because of her stubborn will, but then we discovered that Bu thought that a curse had been put on her, and that there was nothing she could do about it. She felt that if she ate or drank anything she would die. But Bu did die, apparently from starvation and fear.

Love understands – or attempts to – the particular needs of the people to whom we are ministering. Once I was visiting Amar where I had previously lived, and a lady begged me to return and live with them. I asked her why. "Because," she answered, "when you are not here we never have any fishhooks." A young man said to me, "If you really care for us you will give us a volleyball." Many times our love is not received, is misunderstood, and at the least not appreciated; but it should not affect our love for them.

If we are to love lost people – especially people from a vastly different culture than our own – what will it involve? For me, it has involved learning to eat such unpalatable things as jungle rat, tree kangaroo, lizards, snakes, and even grub worms. I shall never forget my first experience at eating grub worms. I was visiting in a village hut when my good friend, Pemar, took a layer of sago, spread it out on the very dirty bark floor, took three large grubs off the coals, broke them into several pieces with dirty hands, squeezed the "juice" onto the sago, wrapped the worms in it like a jelly roll, and proudly handed it to me. People in any culture appreciate it when we eat their food, and the Citak people certainly are no exception. Sometimes the food they offer is palatable, but unsanitary or unhealthy, such as wild pork which has not been cooked properly.

Once a headhunter, Bidaw had one jungle fruit he wanted to divide for my friend Gail Vinje and me. He peeled it with a dirty axe, and divided it the simplest way he knew – he bit it in half. I got the half that came out of his mouth. On another occasion, a young fellow "told on his friend" by reporting to me that his friend had brushed his teeth for the first time in his life with my toothbrush, three days previously. It was a long time before I would enjoy brushing my teeth again. Loving lost people can mean deliberately exposing ourselves to such things.

Sometimes it involves enduring unpleasant conditions such as being bitten by strange bugs in the mats, having flies swarm over your food, being "felt" by people not used to white skin, or having them search for lice in your head with dirty hands while you are praying that they won't find any. For me, it has involved having naked men sit on my dining table, or lie down on my living room couch. It has meant "sleeping" in village huts or in unsteady houses.

Loving the lost has sometimes meant having absolutely no privacy, not even to bathe or to change clothes. My friend, Ruth Dougherty and I were taking a bath fully clothed in a dirty river once when Pau, the village chief, who had collected the skulls of six men after killing and eating them, took possibly his first bath along with us. We learned to change clothes quite effectively under a sheet.

We pitched tents once when visiting some of the villages during very hot and humid weather. A group of men built several fires in front of the tent opening, and sat up all night talking and guarding us. The last thing we saw before going to sleep, and the first thing we saw in the morning were the faces of men watching us "sleep".

Exposing ourselves to disease and danger is also part of living out love. During the past 20 years in Irian Jaya, the missionary community has averaged over one missionary death a year, mostly from airplane crashes. The only mode of transportation into most of the area is a single engine airplane which flies over very rugged terrain and changing weather patterns. I have had ameba, other intestinal parasites, fractured spine, broken heel, and I lost count as to the number of malaria attacks.

In February, 1983, my friend Gail Vinje, Citak Christians Sahu and Yakub Fiak, and I were almost killed by some very primitive people in the Brazza River area. It was a very frightening experience for all of us. But just a few days after we were evacuated from the area, Sahu said to me, "Just because they were about to kill us doesn't mean that we can just forget them. We must go back and tell them God's Word."

Our lifestyles may have to be drastically changed to translate God's love through our lives to lost people. So what should motivate us? Dwelling on God's love for us and thinking daily about the price He paid to show His love for us. We must realize that the opportunity of sharing His love with lost people is glorious, not an obligation. We can never adequately show lost people what God's love is like, but it is an honor to attempt it, however inadequate it may be.

The joy of watching the Holy Spirit open people's hearts to understand and accept God's love is worth whatever "sacrifice" we may have to make. To realize that God chose sinful, imperfect and unworthy people like ourselves to show His perfect love to lost people should cause us to discard the word "sacrifice". As we grow in our understanding of His love for us, and in our love for Him, we should be grateful for the privilege of loving lost people for Him.

In this book you will meet many of these precious people living in the dense jungle rain forests of Papua,

Indonesia. You will learn about how they went from naked cannibals, without the Bible or the ability to read, to 23 churches, and having the New Testament in their language. The journey was sometimes funny, sometimes frustrating, sometimes discouraging, sometimes dangerous, but always rewarding.

But first, what is a missionary?

Chapter 1

WHAT IS A MISSIONARY?

"Go ye into all the world, and preach the gospel to every creature." Mark 16:15

Once when I was visiting a church I had the privilege of speaking to a Sunday school class which was made up of mentally challenged adults. It was such a neat experience, and I am so thankful for that opportunity! One gentleman in the class was very animated and kept saying, "I'm smart!"

After teaching the lesson I asked the students, "Who knows what a missionary does?" The same gentleman waved his hands excitedly and said, "I know. I'm smart!" "All right, what does a missionary do?" I asked. He stuck his chest out and proudly announced, "They get the offering."

I fear that is the way we come across more than we realize. We go into a church, tell stories about weird places and strange people, quote Scripture and sing a song in a foreign language, and get the offering.

What really is a missionary?

I prefer to stick to the definition I had as a child growing up in Sunday school. A missionary is, "Someone who goes around the world to tell people about Jesus."

So what makes a person a missionary? A missionary is a person who is called and sent by God. Some would say that I have oversimplified it, but I think that it is, indeed, just that simple. God loves every person in the world and died for every one of them. He commanded us to go and tell them the good news. He chose certain individuals to be His ambassadors, and we should never forget what an honor and privilege that is.

Once after I had given my testimony to the girls in a Bible College, I asked if anyone had a question. One young lady stood and said something like this, "I have many talents. I sing and play several instruments. I can draw and paint. Can my talents be used on the mission field?"

My immediate impulse was to answer, "No, not until you realize where your talents came from and until you are willing to allow God to use them, or not to use them, as He sees fit."

Looking at missionaries who have been used by God, you will see that they are all so very different. Some have many talents, others have very few. Some are highly qualified from the world's point of view, while others aren't. Some are orators, and others can hardly introduce themselves to a crowd. All kinds of personalities are represented. ALL have been called by God, and He supplies what they need to be His ambassadors to do the job that He has planned for them.

None of us can boast, and none of us can claim any merit. All of us must be eternally grateful for the honor and privilege God gave us by calling us to serve him as missionaries.

Chapter 2

ROAD TO NEW GUINEA/WEST IRIAN/IRIAN JAYA/PAPUA

" How did you know that God had called you to the mission field?" That is a question I often hear when speaking to young people. If there is a married lady in the audience I will ask her, "How did you know that you were in love with your husband?" The response is amusing. She normally will squirm around on her seat, grunt, wave her arms around, and finally say something like this, "I don't know how I knew. I just knew."

My response is, "That's it. You will just know." I "just knew" at the age of 12 that God had called me to be a missionary. I had never seen a missionary at the time, but had read books about missionaries who lived in the 1800s. I had seen pictures of them. They all had long hair tied up in a bun on top of their head. They wore faded print dresses that came down to their ankles, and wore brogan shoes. I used to think, "I am going to be just like that!"

The first missionary I ever saw was at summer camp. An elderly retired missionary lady was there, and she looked just like the pictures I had seen in the books. She would sit out in front of her cabin in a rocking chair and I would sit on the steps and just stare at her with admiration. I had a longing to be just like her.

God put a burning desire in my heart to be a missionary. But there were hurdles to overcome.

HURDLE NO. 1

"But my God shall supply all your need according to His riches in glory by Christ Jesus." Phil. 4:19

I needed to learn the truth found in that verse, and God in His infinite wisdom sent experiences to help me.

HOW TO GO TO BIBLE COLLEGE WITH NOTHING

I was the fourth of six children with no father, who had died when I was eight years old. My mother worked very hard just to keep the family together. We lived in the country so we had plenty to eat. We had cows, chickens, and pigs and always had a big garden. Just in our yard we had apples, pears, peaches, cherries, figs, and grapes. Blackberries, plums, raspberries, muscadines and huckleberries grew wild. Although we ate well, there was no money for other things.

At that time nobody in the country community where I grew up had ever gone to college. I came along as one of the poorest kids around, talking about going to Bible College. One day my mother forbade me to talk about it anymore. She said, "I will get you through High School, and then you are on your own." Believe me, she meant it. She needed to get some of us out of the house. Although I didn't talk about it again, I sure thought a lot about it. I would often cry myself to sleep begging God to let me be a missionary. I would pray, "I will do anything. I will go anywhere. I will die for You. Just please let me be a missionary." It seemed impossible.

My mother kept her word. I graduated from High School on Thursday, and Mom moved me out the next Thursday. Being a country girl, we hardly ever went to the "big" city of Greenville, so when Mom moved me into the YWCA, I was terrified. I was 17 years old and had never been away from home except for summer camp. Amazingly, I got a job at the age of 17 as a Medical Secretary in the local hospital. With God's help and hard work, I worked my way through Bible College and finished in four years, but not without its challenges.

WILL I BE FIRED?

I was an eighteen year old smart aleck. My job at the hospital was to take the doctors' orders, order the medicines from the pharmacy, send lab requests to the lab, and prepare the orders for the nurses to give the medicines. There were certain procedures that I was to follow with new patients. Quite often the doctor would call in the admitting orders before the patient arrived. If he had not called them, then I would call the doctor after the patient arrived. Sometimes the admitting doctor would want to call in a specialist. Either he would call that doctor himself, or he would order me to do so. Of course, I could not call in another doctor without the order from the admitting doctor.

One night two couples showed up. One of the ladies was the patient. I was preparing to call the admitting doctor when one of the men – not the patient's husband – came up to the desk and demanded that I call a surgeon whose name he gave me. Knowing that the admitting doctor very likely did indeed want to consult the surgeon, I told the man that I would call the admitting doctor for the order. The rude man spoke really rough, and told me in no uncertain terms that the patient had appendicitis, and that it would be my fault if she died!

Remember, I was an eighteen year old smart aleck and didn't enjoy being yelled at, when I was trying to explain that all I had to do was call the admitting doctor first. While all this was going on, I noticed that the nurses all exited the nurses' station, leaving me alone with the delightful man. Doctors coming that way would suddenly turn away and disappear. I wondered a bit about who in the world this rude man was.

He said, "Call Mr. Toomey." Mr. Robert Toomey was none less than the hospital administrator. I had never even spoken to him. It was about 8 o'clock at night and he was at home. "Fine," I said. As soon as he answered, Mr. Rude had come around the corner of the nurses' station, and yanked the phone out of my hand. He said, "Hello, Bob." I thought, "I'm dead."

Mr. Rude shoved the phone into my hand, and Mr. Toomey very politely asked if he could take over! Wow! Of course I said yes, and hung up the phone and went about my work. Mr. Rude said, "Well, are you going to call the surgeon?" "Nope," I replied.

By that time it was time for me to go off duty. When I returned the next day I learned that the surgeon operated and removed a normal appendix. It turned out that Mr. Rude was just the Chairman of the Chamber of Commerce, a very powerful and wealthy man who channeled lots of money to the hospital. He had a reputation for being rude, but nobody else could afford to respond, so I was the heroine that day. However, I was told by several doctors that I would probably be fired. Some of them offered me a job if I did get fired.

When I saw the Director of Nurses coming my direction I thought, "This is it." Mr. Rude had indeed written a letter demanding that I be fired. The Director of Nurses said that I had done what a lot of people had wanted to do, and that I had been right. I could not have called the surgeon without an order from the admitting doctor, so I would not be fired.

Now to show you what a delightful sense of humor God has, shortly after that incident Mr. Rude's wife came into my speech class at the university. She was called on to give speeches and was going to monitor the class. Of course, I did not tell her about the incident with her husband. She was a lovely lady and we all enjoyed having her in the class.

About that time, I had an unexpected financial problem which necessitated my dropping out of school for a semester. My first day out of school I received a call from the finance office asking me if I would return to school if my tuition for that semester were paid. Of course, I said yes. Guess who paid my school bill? You guessed it, Mr. Rude's wife!

I lived in fear of running into the two of them together and him learning that not only did I not get fired, but that he – through his wife – paid my tuition for that semester. I learned that God can supply my need from the most unexpected source.

HURDLE NO. 2
OPPOSITION

I wrote this in my diary in April, 1962: "Some women told Jean yesterday that they didn't believe that God calls single girls to the mission field. Well, I've only to answer to God. I do not doubt that He has called me and unless He does call single girls, then I had better find a husband."

Another person in my church advised my pastor to not allow me to go. That was a theme that continued to come up again and again over the years, but I "just knew" that God had called me. God had called me, I was single, and I did go, and stayed for over 40 years.

Some of the world's greatest people have been lonely men and women who committed themselves to the hand of God.
–Lee Roberson

HUDDLE NO. 3
LESSONS IN FAITH
CAR STOLEN

After two years, I transferred to Tennessee Temple University in Chattanooga, Tennessee where I worked at a small private hospital. I owned a 1948 Chevrolet which I used to drive back and forth between the campus and the hospital. One night I came out from work at 11 o'clock p.m. and my car, named "Alfalfa," was gone. We called the police and made a report, and someone took me to the campus. The police said that if they found the car, it would no doubt be stripped down.

Our dorm was a house. It was against the rules for me to be out of bed, but since everyone else was asleep, no one knew I was up. Without a car I could not work. If I could not work, I could not pay my tuition, which meant that I could not go to school. I went across into the living room and was reading my Bible, crying and praying. I went to sleep with my face in my Bible. Around 4 a.m. the police called and told me that they had found my car, and if I would come for it, I could avoid towing charges. Another girl had a car and I woke her up, then woke up the dorm mother for permission, and we ended up with a car load of girls all excited about having some fun. The car had been found unharmed in a very dark part of Chattanooga near the railroad tracks. Was I ever glad to have Alfalfa back.

BILLFOLD STOLEN

It was three days before Christmas. I had to work Christmas day, but had planned to go home for several days after Christmas. I had just enough money to pay the school bill, buy gas for the car, plus a few dollars to buy my mother a Christmas gift. I was writing a term paper on the subject of faith. I took all the money I had saved up, put it in my billfold, and on the way to pay the bill I stopped by the library for some books on faith. I laid the books and billfold down to look through the card catalog, and someone stole the billfold with every cent of money I had except for 25 cents I had in my pocket.

It wasn't completely a matter of becoming discouraged and wanting to quit – I had no choice. I wanted to quit immediately but couldn't. I didn't have money for gas. I was one discouraged kid when I showed up to work. I thought, I will work until payday and then go home. Word went around the hospital and patients began giving me money.

Then a day or so later, I received a phone call from Luther Massingill from WDEF radio in Chattanooga. He was a fine Christian man who was well known by about everyone but me. I never had time to listen to the radio so didn't know him. He had heard about what had happened, announced it on the radio, and I got back more than I had lost. Luther became a great friend and helped me a lot in getting ready to go to the field.

God was doing His thing in preparing me for what He had for me in the future. I probably would not have done it that way. No doubt, had I been arranging things,

I would have had some wealthy benefactor show up and pay my tuition so I could just study. God in His wisdom knew that I had much to learn, and He sent the experiences I needed to grow in faith and to trust Him.

HURDLE NO. 4
WHERE, LORD?

"I'll go where You want me to go, dear Lord."

I knew that God had called me to be a missionary, but where would that be? God had put in my heart to go to primitive people, but I didn't know where that was. In Bible College I met lots of missionaries. One would speak to the students and I would think, "Maybe I will go there." The next week another missionary would come and I would think, "Perhaps I will go there." This continued for a long time and I didn't "just know" where I was to go. I was asking God to show me.

Then I went home for a short vacation, and a missionary from my home church was home from a place called Dutch New Guinea. I had never heard of that country. He and his wife were at a place called Senggo, which was inhabited by the Citak tribe in the rain forests of the south coast of the island of Dutch New Guinea. The people wore no clothes and had just recently stopped practicing cannibalism. The missionary wife had made bright red drawstring shorts for some of the little boys. They showed a slide of those little boys playing in the village. Remember these little boys in their red shorts as they will come up again later in this book.

I was just sitting there "in the way" looking at those cute little boys in their bright red shorts when seemingly out from nowhere came this thought, "That is where you are going." From that moment on, I "just knew" where I was to go and never doubted it.

I began looking on the map to find where it was and reading information about the country. I learned that it belonged to the Netherlands, but that Indonesia was agitating to have it turned over to them.

I also began looking for a Mission Board with work there and found only three that I could consider.

I wrote this in my diary in April, 1962: "Wish I could leave now! Lord, teach me patience. I want a greater burden for lost souls here as well as in New Guinea. Lord, don't let me go just for adventure or excitement, but let it be for Jesus' sake only. I can't take the discouragements of the mission field for the sake of excitement, but I can endure it all for Jesus sake, for one day He will say, "Well done," if I am faithful.

May 5, 1962 I wrote: "I feel a need to continually search my heart for motives for service. I pray that my motive for any service will be to do the will of my Lord Jesus Christ."

Finally, I finished Bible College and applied to the Mission Board.

HURDLE NO. 5
WILL THE MISSION BOARD REALLY ACCEPT ME?

It was with fear and trembling that I sent my application to the Mission Board. I thought, "They will never accept me." It was a very detailed process, and by the time they were finished there was nothing they did not know about the applicant. They had transcripts from schools, as well as references from my pastor, the school, my roommates, etc. Then they asked those people to send them the names of several more people.

I will never forget the day I received a letter from the Board inviting me to come to Chicago, Illinois for Candidate School. I knew that the invitation to Candidate School meant that I was most likely going to be accepted – but that would not come until after the month in Candidate School. I tried hard to be on my very best behavior, because I figured that they were watching every move and listening to every word.

Meeting the Medical Director was a terrifying experience. He never smiled.

Then came the time when I had to meet the Board of Directors. They asked questions about what I believed. I had already submitted all of that in writing, but guess they wanted to hear me say it. I knew what I believed but was too scared to say it. One of the men would ask a question, and another one would apparently feel sorry for me and answer it. I don't recall answering any of their questions.

Amazingly, I was given that coveted letter of acceptance. I could hardly believe that the board had actually accepted ME. On the way home on the bus I read the letter over and over until I had memorized every word of it. I kept thinking, "They accepted me! I am going to be a missionary!"

HURDLE NO. 6
DO I REALLY HAVE TO DO DEPUTATION?

Standing in front of anyone scared me half to death. Then if I had to say anything, it was almost worse than death. I knew how to work for what I needed, but asking churches and people to support me? Never!

Dr. Lee Roberson at Tennessee Temple University offered to help me get started. He wrote a letter of recommendation to every Temple graduate in the state of

Florida. I went down one side of Florida and up the other side visiting churches and did not get one cent of support. First of all, I knew almost nothing about New Guinea and was too scared to even tell what I did know. My standard answer to most questions was, "I don't know."

I have no idea how I got my support, but have a feeling that the pastors figured that if they didn't help me, I never would get it. I did get it and began preparing to go to the field. I was SO excited.

My support came in. We had to take with us literally everything we would need for the next four years as nothing was available on the island. Imagine trying to decide how much toilet paper you will need for four years.

I got my outfit together, packed it in 55 gallon steel drums, had the lids welded on and I was ready to go.

But there was one more major hurdle.

HURDLE NO. 7
A CHANGE IN GOVERNMENTS AND REJECTED VISA

Indonesia took over control of Dutch New Guinea and the U.N. moved in for a year during the transition. My visa application, along with three others, were the first ones to go in under the Indonesian government.

Since we had no idea what would happen with the visa application the mission wrote a letter to me requesting that I come to Chicago and work at headquarters while we waited. I definitely did not want to go to Chicago. I wanted desperately to go to what had become Irian Barat or West Irian.

I arrived in Chicago on Saturday and went to church on Sunday with a friend who worked at headquarters. She taught a children's class and I went to an adult class. When I introduced myself to the teacher he said, "Oh, did you know that your visa has been rejected?"

I was speechless. After Sunday school I asked my friend about it and she responded with, "Who told you?" The word had come on Friday and the men at headquarters were going to break the news gently to me on Monday, but the teacher had blurted it out in Sunday school. I was devastated. I was confused. I was absolutely certain that God had let me know that I was to go to West Irian. Now the Indonesian government was saying that they did not want any more missionaries there.

The General Director called me in and told me about how Paul had wanted to go to Bithynia but was not allowed to do so. Dr. Roberson at Tennessee Temple wrote to me and "encouraged" me with the story about how Paul had wanted to go to Bithynia. My pastor, Dr. Harold Sightler, wrote to me and reminded me that Paul had wanted to go to Bithynia. I wanted to scream, "I DON'T WANT TO GO TO BITHYNIA!"

The men at headquarters told me that obviously God had not wanted me to go to West Irian. When I argued, they said that if God had called me to West Irian, then I would be on my way, but the door had apparently closed. What they said made sense, but I could not reconcile it with the absolute certainty that I had felt when I "just knew" that I was to go to West Irian.

I cried every day for about three months. Anytime the word "visa" was mentioned, it set me off again. Often in morning chapel times when the word "visa" was mentioned, I would hear someone whisper, "There she goes again."

The missionaries in Indonesia were trying to convince the government there to reconsider. It appeared that they would not do so. The mission asked me to consider going to Taiwan. It did not interest me in the least. I had been so positive that God had called me to West Irian. If I were wrong about that, how could I ever know God's will?

I had been given some brochures about Taiwan to read. I was in my room one night and started to read them. In utter frustration I tore them up and threw them into the trash. Moody Radio Station was playing my favorite mission song, "So Send I You." When I heard the verse that said, "So send I you to leave your life's ambition," I became very alert. My life's ambition was to be a missionary. Was God telling me that He did not want me to be a missionary?

All my life had been directed at one goal – to be a missionary. I had never even considered anything else. I was totally convinced that God had wanted me in West Irian, but the door was closed. No other country appealed to me. I had never been so confused in my life.

That night I fought probably the biggest battle of my life. I was not ready to face the possibility that God may not want me to be a missionary. After some time of bitter tears, soul searching, and finally surrender, I prayed, "God, did you really let me work so hard to go to college, get my support, and pack my drums while it never was your will that I be a missionary? Are you really saying that you want me to leave my life's ambition to be a missionary? I want to be a missionary. I will always want to be a missionary. But if you don't want me to be a missionary, then don't let me go. I want your will." Then I fell asleep.

The next morning I was sitting at my desk when one of the men came to where I was, and placed a telegram from Indonesia out on my desk. It read, "Stringer visa being reconsidered." I won't try to explain the excitement that I showed, but it was pretty undignified. My excitement was immediately squelched when he said, "Don't get excited. You don't understand some of these countries. You can't get excited until you see the visa stamped in your passport." I settled down and went back to work.

About two weeks later the same man came bearing another telegram that read, "Stringer visa granted." I said a simple, "Thank you," and went back to work. I noticed that he looked a bit strange, but he had already told me not to get excited if I did not see it stamped in my passport. It wasn't in my passport, was it? It was almost 15 minutes later when it actually sank in – that telegram said "granted". I went running through the office, gave my notice effective immediately, and started out to return to my room to pack.

The General Director called me in, and would you believe that he began by talking about how Paul had wanted to go to Bithynia? Then he read on where Paul had gone to Macedonia in God's will, and ended up being beaten and in jail. A real encourager. He said, "We don't know what will happen. The visa is granted for one year. We don't know what the future is for missionary work in West Irian, but I think we can know one thing for sure. God called you to West Irian." I am sure you are wondering what my response was. It was, "I told you so."

God was so good to give me that experience. Otherwise I could have arrived on the field, and when the tough experiences came, Satan could have said, "It was all your idea. You wanted to come. God had nothing to do with it." The tough experiences did come, but when they did I KNEW that if I quit I would have been out of God's will. For over 40 years I never doubted that I was there in God's will.

FINAL HURDLE OVER – WEST IRIAN OR BUST

From my diary on July 4, 1964: "I searched my heart again tonight for any motive in my going to West Irian other than the constraining love of Christ. I love Him dearly."

July 13, 1964: "Visited family and friends – some for the last time before I leave. This could be the last time I will ever see some of them alive. God is giving His marvelous grace during these days of sorrow as I have to say goodbye to the ones I love most on this earth."

July 15, 1964: "Tonight at church I gave a few words of farewell and thanks to the greatest friends I will ever have. Thank God for them. I'll never look back."

Thursday, July 18, 1964: "This is the day when my daydreams of many years become a reality. Thank God! The Lord has given me a real peace, such as I have never before experienced. I don't feel too sad about leaving, but am really looking forward to it. Had prayer with my pastor just before boarding the plane. Waved goodbye and on my way. Last sight showed all waving. Thank God for them."

In San Francisco: "As I board this airplane in a few minutes I don't know what the future holds, but I know Him who holds the future and leave it all to Him. "The love of Christ constrains me." I know this is God's will. Thanks to Him for His marvelous and wonderful peace at this time. His grace is sufficient."

The final hurdle had been passed and I was on my way. I had never been on an airplane but was so excited that I was on my way to the field. I kept thinking, "I am a missionary! I am a missionary! I really am a missionary!"

We talk a lot about surrendering to do God's will." I believe that we should be standing in line hoping and praying that God will choose us to do something special for Him. He chooses us not because we are someone special or that we have any special ability. He doesn't choose us because we have somehow become worthy. He chooses us because of His amazing grace and tender mercy. When He chooses us to do something for Him we have been highly honored and should thank Him every day for that privilege.

Chapter 3

I AM A MISSIONARY

I am convinced that there has never been a missionary who was more excited about it that I was.

Most people, I am sure, never expected me to last. I did not fit the widely accepted profile of what a missionary should be like. But one thing I knew. God had called me and I was thrilled about it.

When missionaries would come to speak to the students in Bible College it seemed that they all had stories about rats, snakes, insects, and all kinds of weird foods. I wanted it all!

My first house was a kingstrand – heavy corrugated aluminum. If you want to know what that felt like in the tropics, just turn your oven up to about 120 degrees and get in it.

My first house

It had not been lived in for several years, and although the missionaries there had cut the grass around it, they had not evicted the residents. Nor could they, since the "windows" were torn screens. The house had become a haven for large jungle rats along with a variety of other critters. I would lie in bed and watch the rats parade right through the open windows. I borrowed a large rat trap from another missionary and caught seven rats in one night and did not even scratch the surface. I was SO excited! Missionaries have rats. I have rats. I am a missionary!

A couple of days after arrival on the field I looked up to see the largest spider I had ever seen sitting serenely on the wall. I decided to swat it. When I started to swat it, the thing jumped right at me! It took a while for me to recover, but when I did, was I ever excited. Not only did I have spiders, I had attack spiders.

Food? No problem. If they can eat it, I can. Bring it on.

But my reason for going to West Irian was to tell the people about Jesus. I realized that I could not tell them a thing since I did not know their language. I wanted to learn their language.

Chapter 4

KOKONAO – MIMIKA TRIBE

After working in The Missions Fellowship office for a year, I finally arrived at my first assignment – Kokonao in the Mimika tribe.

I was anxious to begin learning the Indonesian language and then on to studying the Mimika language.

It was October 1, 1965. I was unpacking my suitcase when the missionary living across the yard came running out to inform us that the Communists had taken over the country in a coup. They had taken over the radio and announced that they were in control. My first thought was, "I haven't even learned the language and now I will be thrown out of the country." By a miraculous chain of events the military turned the coup around, and hundreds of communists were killed and missionaries got to stay.

Marge Smith and I lived together in another aluminum house along with a variety of critters including roaches, rats, frogs, etc. Dogs and chickens also came and went as they pleased. I remember how Marge would clean the bathroom shelves. First of all, she would catch a couple of chickens and bring them into the house. Then she would remove the toilet paper, etc. Dozens of roaches would come scampering out running all directions while the chickens enjoyed a feast.

Speaking of chickens enjoying a feast, we had at least one hungry chicken. I was sitting on the ground in the back yard peeling the outer husk off a coconut with a hatchet. We fed the chickens coconut, so they were standing around waiting for lunch. I accidently hit my thumb, chopping off the end. It went flying across the yard where a lucky chicken quickly gobbled it down before checking it out. Having the end cut off of ones thumb was not a lot of fun. I could not bear having a bandage on it, and the flies thought that was great. Marge made a "cage" out of chicken wire, put it over my thumb, and wrapped gauze around it. Where there is a will there is a way.

The frogs became my biggest challenge. I named them "Freddie the Frog." The house did not have a ceiling so they had free run of the house. They loved to space themselves around the house and conduct loud discussions among themselves in the night. They often would perch themselves right over my bed and croak like Gabriel's trumpet at about 5 a.m. I would search for them in the daytime and throw them all outside, only to have them return with all their friends after dark.

One morning we woke up to find red frog foot prints all over the kitchen – cabinets, floor, and walls. A frog had turned over a bottle of mercurochrome and gotten in it.

Marge was a calm, easy going, person, and *never* panicked. She loved any kind of animal, and would not allow me to abuse even the least of them. She did allow me to swat flies and mosquitoes.

One day I was in the living room studying Indonesian. Marge was cleaning out the pantry. I heard "Whoops." That was a panic attack for Marge. A rat had jumped off the top shelf, run down her shift dress, around her waist, and down to the floor. I hate to even try to imagine what I would have done. Typically, Marge said, "It just went through. I figured it would find its way out." Oh, to be like her!

Since Indonesia had not controlled West Irian long, lots of receptions, etc. were done to instill patriotic feeling into the Irianese people. It seemed that we had flag raising ceremonies almost weekly followed by receptions with lots of boring speeches. We were expected to attend. It was good for language learning though.

Marge and I participated in many of these. The government decided that we needed a community ladies' group, and that we must learn to march and participate in the flag raising ceremony. We amused everyone with our marching.

I was a long way from being fluent in Indonesian. A Muslim soldier was teaching us to march. As the tallest woman was always in front, that meant that Marge and I, being the tallest women there, led the march. Marge would often whisper the orders in English for me.

One day we were marching down the path and the soldier was marching along on my left. Marge was on my right. The soldier yelled, "Turn right!" Everyone turned right except me. I turned left right into the soldier, much to the delight of all the ladies. He was not too happy.

We were required to wear old uniforms left over from the Dutch. Dutchmen were very large and the uniforms definitely did not fit us. We were not allowed to cut them, but could roll up the sleeves, which we rolled up as far as they would go, but they were still below our elbows. Then there were the hats! They also were several sizes too large for us. We were trained to march past the government dignitaries at the flag raising ceremony, and to turn our heads to face them as the order to "salute" was given as we passed. Our heads turned, but our hats kept facing forward! We had a lot of fun!

Ibu Kartini was a lady recognized as having achieved emancipation for the women of Indonesia. Once a year they celebrate Ibu Kartini Day. Marge and I wore the

Indonesian sarong and marched in the flag raising ceremony. The sarong was tight around our ankles, and staying in step while jumping a ditch created quite an attraction. That night they had a reception. I had written a song for Marge and me to the tune of "Home On The Range". Neither Marge nor I could sing, which added to the entertainment. When we were called to the platform we discovered that we could not go up the steps wearing the tight sarong, so we had to crawl up on hands and knees. We had a coconut and a crab with us which we held up at the appropriate time during the song. It was awful singing, but we brought the house down, and after it was all over a Muslim lady said to me, "We didn't think the missionaries could be that much fun."

Here is the famous song:

"Duduk ditepi Sungai"
Kami mau pergi ke Kokonao
Dan tinggal selamanya
Dan minum kelapa
Dan makan keraka
Dan dukuk ditepi sungai.
Kami suka berbaris, dengan kaum Perwib
Dengan maju, jalan, dan siap.
Tapi yang terbaik, itu istirahat
Dan duduk ditepi sungai.
Chorus
Oh, Kokonao
Kota yang bagus dan indah
Mana tidak pernah hati susah apa
Kota yang tercinta kami.

"Sitting on the edge of the river"
We want to go to Kokonao
And live forever
And drink coconut
And eat crabs
And sit on the edge of the river
We like to march with the ladies
With forward, march, and ready
But what is best, is rest
And sit on the edge of the river
Chorus
Oh, Kokonao
Town which is nice and beautiful.
Where there is never any trouble
Town that we love.

I was studying Indonesian, beginning to teach a children's class in Indonesian, and teaching an English class. The English class included two protestants, four catholic teachers, three muslims including the imam. I enjoyed that class.

We had a desire to analyze the Mimika language and learn it. Being the government post several dialects of the Mimika language were spoken at Kokonao. In order to effectively analyze the language we needed to work with only one dialect so moved to the outlying village of Amar. I lived there until 1974.

Chapter 5

AMAR

MORE FROGS

We caught rain water off the roof in 55 gal. drums which sat on a tower under the roof. Then it ran into the house by gravity. One night in the middle of the night a frog was keeping me awake croaking near the drums. I didn't want to wake Marge, so got up in my pajamas, and sneaked out of the house – found a ladder and climbed up on the tower. I found the frog, but had forgotten to take a stick with me so decided to use my flashlight to knock the frog down. However, instead of hopping off, the frog grabbed hold of the flashlight. I let out a scream and slung the flashlight along with the frog across the yard.

Now the funny part was Marge. Remember, Marge never panics. At least she never had before that. She came running out the back door shining her flashlight all around the yard yelling, "Where are you? Where are you?" Of course, I was sitting up on the water tower, in the dark, laughing my head off. I couldn't see how to get down because I had thrown my flashlight away. Marge threatened to leave me there until daylight.

She told me later that when she saw me at 2:00 a.m. in my pajamas, on the water tower screaming, she thought I had gone crazy! Perhaps I had.

MEDICAL CLINIC

One thing that I have never had any desire to do was medical work. I did work in two hospitals when I worked my way through Bible College, but that was a necessity. I never wanted to do anything that had anything to do with nursing. However, when Marge and I moved to the village of Amar there was no medical help of any kind. I think it is so neat how God prepares us for what He has for us to do. I went to Pirimapun where our missionary doctor and wife, Ken and Sylvia Dresser, served. They taught me a lot, including how to give shots. I got my "doctor's degree" in about two weeks.

With my "diploma" in my hand I returned to Amar and opened a small medical clinic and began treating the sick. Fortunately, I had the luxury of being able to call Ken and Sylvia on the single-side band radio for advice when I needed it.

The Mimika people, as well as the Citak people, had a very frustrating thing which they did when someone was very sick or unconscious. They would pick up a red hot coal and burn them. They said it "made their eyes bright." It did that for sure if they had any life in them at all. I noticed that most of the adults had burn scars on their jaws and wondered what that was. I learned that they had burned themselves when they had a toothache. I also learned that they would cut an aching tooth out with a knife. Something must be done about that!

Ken came and gave me a few pointers and I took my pliers out of my tool box and added a new dimension to the medical program – pulling teeth. The people loved having their teeth pulled and would look in each other's mouths looking for teeth that they might talk me into pulling.

I remember one poor man who came with a tooth-ache. I pulled and pulled and couldn't get the tooth out, so I sent him home expecting never to see him again.

However, he returned the next day. Again, it wouldn't budge no matter how hard I tried so I sent him home again. The third day I was determined to get it out. I had him stand on the ground and I stood on the top step high above him and pulled with all my might. When it did finally come out, I almost knocked his upper tooth out with it. He was thrilled. So was I. Oh yes, Novocain? Not a bit. Believe me, pulling teeth with pliers and no anesthetic was an act of mercy considering how they did it!

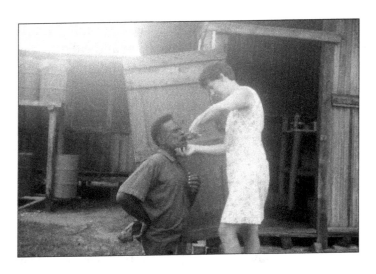

Pulling teeth

Once while on furlough I showed slides of my teeth pulling episodes in a supporting church and a dentist was in the audience! I think he almost passed out! He informed me in no uncertain terms that, "You can't do that!" I informed him that he had just seen my pictures proving him wrong.

He invited me to spend two weeks there and he called the local prison. They sent up their prisoners and I pulled their teeth – with dental forceps! Wow! What a difference an instrument makes. One giant of a man looked up at me and said, "Can she pull teeth?" The dentist said, "Oh yes, she has pulled lots of teeth." He omitted the fact that I had pulled them with pliers.

I returned to the field with my lovely set of dental forceps and a good time was had by all.

EXPERT PLACENTA DELIVERER

I had never delivered a baby and dreaded the day when they would have a complication and call me to "do something." They normally took care of deliveries themselves for which I was thankful.

Then one day it happened. They called me not to deliver the baby, but for a retained placenta. I prayed all the way wondering what in the world I was going to do when I got there.

When I arrived the mother was sitting on a palm branch and because of all their taboos I was not allowed to touch a thing. I wondered why they had called me, if they were not going to allow me to do anything – as if I knew what to do anyway. I looked the situation over and prayed again, and then suggested that the lady get up off the palm branch. Her look said, "Do you know what you are doing?" Of course, I had no idea what I was doing. She reluctantly followed my instructions and got up off the palm branch in a squatting position. When she did that a very big miracle happened. The placenta fell out! I was the hero, and the great miracle worker. I went home with a skip to my walk, glorying over all the praise I was getting from the people who had observed me perform the miracle.

After that very often when a lady had a baby they would call me to "deliver the placenta." It was a long time before I ever actually delivered a baby, but I chalked up lots of experience by "delivering" several placentas.

Ken had told me that if I ever had a hand presentation to call the airplane immediately. Normally we would have to have his permission before calling an emergency, but this one did not need prior approval. That was because he said that there was nothing that I could do and the patient would have to evacuate immediately in order to save the mother's life. I dreaded the day that would happen and hoped that it never would.

Then it happened. One day I was called to the village and there was a hand presentation! The Mimika people never wanted to leave their village or tribe for anything. Often they would prefer to die rather than leave their village. I told them that the baby would most likely die, and in order to try to save the life of the mother I was calling an emergency flight and returned home to do so. Shortly thereafter someone came to my door and said that the baby was delivered. The baby had already died and people had cut the baby apart and had gotten it out. That was so hard for me and I felt that I had failed them. I gave the mother lots of penicillin and she recovered.

ALCOHOL IN MERCUROCHROM

The daily medical clinics had become so time con-suming as the people, especially the children, would line up every morning with small scratches. Often they would scratch off the scab to make it bleed so I would treat it. They would be VERY dirty and I would order them to go and wash the hand, foot, or whatever had the injury. They would return with just the spot where the scratch was wet. No need to wash any more than I demanded.

Normally I would put mercurochrome on their scratches. Then one day I thought up a wonderful thing – I thought – which would discourage a lot of the "patients." I put alcohol in the mercurochrome, thinking that they would not like that at all. So the next morning when they lined up with their small scratches, I began to put a liberal amount of mercurochrome mixed with rubbing alcohol on them. I expected that the ones in line would suddenly disappear when the first ones began jumping around and blowing their sores. The reaction was definitely not what I had expected. They did indeed jump up and down and run around the yard blowing on their sores, but to my surprise and disappointment they loved it. Anything that burned like that has to be good. The more it burned the better they liked it and my clinic time doubled.

I never knew what kind of interesting response I would get when I asked them where they were sick. They would inevitably place the palms of their hands in front of their face and then in one great swoop swipe all the way down to their knees, which being interpreted was, "I am sick all over."

One day a baby from the village of Kawar was brought in with an ear infection with dizziness. The family had burned her really bad to "wake her up." I fussed at them. The next day they called me saying that she was dizzy again. I went out in a solid downpour of rain. The witch doctor was there and was giving her the rub down. The diagnosis? An evil inner ear infection caused by evil spirits of the ear.

The witch doctor would rub the patient from head to foot and attempt to pull out the evil spirit either through the naval, or the toes. I actually saw him pull out the evil spirit in the form of a small stick! However, I saw it in his hand even before he began his "work." He was not very good at the sleight of hand trick.

The people would call the witch doctor first. If he could not cure them, then they would call me. That did not sit too well with me, and if the person was not deathly ill,

I sometimes would leave without treating them. A time or two I chased the witch doctor out of the house.

I gave penicillin to the child, but ran into a problem with her mother. She could not understand why I put the shot in the baby's bottom when it was her ear that was sick! I explained the miracle of the medicine knowing right where the illness was and would go there. By the next morning her ear infection was much better. My penicillin did indeed find the problem in the ear and chased the spirits right out!

One night I was interrupted at about 8 p.m. by folks with their little boy. He had eaten rotten fish "around noon" and was convulsing. He was still alive, but I doubted if he would be alive by morning. They knew that spoiled fish was very dangerous, but for some reason I never understood would eat it knowing that it was spoiled. Albertus, the little boy, survived.

One day an old man came to be treated. He said that he had not urinated in a month! A big glass of water cured him. The following day the chief of the village of Kawar came saying that a man was really sick. He was too ill to walk. He said that when he urinated he went Spsssssssssssssh! I went down to the village to see this wonder and discovered that he was the man who had not urinated in a month. Now he complains that he goes too much. Perhaps he had been drinking too much water? I didn't find anything wrong with him.

A young man came in one morning and wanted me to listen to his toothache with the stethoscope. Another wanted me to "look" at his shoulder with it to see if it was broken.

One day some people brought in a baby with malaria, who had a temperature of 105 degrees. They said that the baby had been convulsing and died! They stuck a safety pin through his ear to "make his eyes bright." It worked and they had brought him back to life by the time they arrived at my house!

It was difficult to make the Mimika people understand medicine. If it did not cure them in one day, they often would not return. Also, if I gave them several days of medicine at one time, they would take it all the first day. On the other hand, sometimes they would return after several days with all the medicine I had given, and would declare that they had taken it every day just like I had told them to. Watching them learn to take pills was an entertainment. They would put the pill in their mouth, drink an entire glass of water, and the pill would still be there. Sometimes it took several glasses of water to wash the pill down.

This was from my diary in 1977: "Treated sores and malaria all day. I longed for even just a few minutes for myself. It is 7 p.m. and the last person has just left."

One day a kid stole his brother's crab and gave it to his father to cook for him. His brother came and saw the crab on the fire and took it. His father picked up a large stick and hit him on the head. Before I could even look at it, the village chief dragged him away to settle the fight. While there they washed the gash with very dirty water! I cleaned it with sterile water and bandaged it and instructed them to bring him back the next day. They said, "We will just use our own medicine." That meant calling the witch doctor.

It was always so very rewarding when I knew that the simple treatments that I did most likely had saved a life. On the other hand, it was just as disappointing when people would die from an illness that I knew could have been cured had they only cooperated.

WITCH DOCTORS AND MIMIKA WITCHCRAFT

Although having had "religion" for about 25 years, they continued to be steeped in witchcraft, witch doctors, curses, and fear. They had been told by the religious leaders that they could worship God and continue with their old beliefs at the same time. At Christmas and Easter they would go into their church for about one-half an hour for "worship" and then have what they called "Second Easter" or "Second Christmas". That meant about two weeks of beating the drums around the clock, dancing in the village and engaging in sex orgies.

When there was some problem in the village the "judge" was often the witch doctor. He had a "special" spear. The people would sit down around him and he would stand in the middle holding the spear. The spear "controlled by the spirits" would move and point right at the guilty person. I often wanted to suggest that he let me hold the spear just to see if it still moved! The initiation ceremony of young boys into adult society also was a wicked ceremony with spirit involvement.

In time, I became friends with the witch doctor and would often tease him offering to buy his magic spear. He began coming to me for medicine when he was sick, and I would offer to trade my medicine for his spear, or "magic" stick. He would just giggle, but accept my medicine. Although I had several opportunities to witness to him, he never accepted Christ.

FEUDING MIMIKAS

The Mimikas loved a good fight. I came to believe that it was just a big game for them. A girl named Paula was promised to Yakob. She went to Kokonao, the government post, and sneaked and married another man. Then they immediately got on the plane for Amoga. That resulted in a BIG fight among the people at Amar which was always exciting to watch and hear.

The women were hilarious as they made all sorts of crazy gestures, ran around screaming, threatening, and saying all kinds of dirty things. I went down and made photos of them, thinking it would embarrass them. It didn't. In fact, they thought it was fun.

The head of the police at Kokonao would periodically send a police to the villages to visit. Those police were Mimikas who had very little training, and very little education, but lots of bravado. Once one of those policemen was at Amar while I was alone on the station. He came to my house and asked for a bar of soap. I told him that I would sell him one. He did not like that. After all, he was the police and I should respect him. I informed him that if he went into one of the stores at Kokonao and wanted a bar of soap, he would pay for it. So why did he think that I would just give it to him.

He had his gun with a bayonet on it. He became VERY angry and pointed his gun at me and threatened me. Then he yanked out the bayonet and slung it on the floor, telling me what he could do with it. I stood my ground just as brave as a person could be, and let him know in no uncertain terms that I was definitely NOT going to GIVE him a bar of soap! Was I stupid? I think I was, but usually they were just loud, but not so brave. He finally turned around to leave and my legs buckled under me and I thought, "He was threatening to kill me."

I called our Field Chairman on the single-side-band radio and the pilot was preparing to come to evacuate me. He was at least 45 minutes away. In the meantime, the police heard that I was talking on the radio and it frightened him, so he was preparing to leave the village. I cancelled the flight, but the police didn't leave because he suddenly became very ill with what was apparently malaria. He was convinced that I had put a curse on him causing the malaria attack. I wanted to give him medicine, but he refused out of fear. He recovered without medicine, and obviously, I didn't have any more trouble with him.

AIRSTRIP VS SOCCER BALL FIELD (BATTLE GROUND)

I imagine that many of you imagine missionaries going out armed with their Bible to learn a foreign language and spend their lives loving the natives and telling them about Jesus. That is how most of us expected it to be when we went to the field. It didn't take much time for us to learn that it just wasn't that simple. Of course, we had to learn the language, and we loved telling the people about Jesus, but there was much more to it.

At Amar, we needed an airstrip in order for the mission plane to land. The pilot could come in on the float plane, but we needed an airstrip for a more economical and easier way to get our supplies in. The big problem was that Amar was very close to the beach, and building an airstrip on sand was a challenge to say the least. Before Marge and I had moved to Amar another missionary had already gone there, had cleared the land for the strip, and had built a house for us. We had our "first landing" and things looked good. So, our biggest challenge was taken care of, so we thought.

Things went well until the rainy season came and our lovely airstrip turned into a swamp and the plane could not land. The only equipment we had to work with were fragile shovels and gunny sacks, and people who had a very bad allergy to work. We had no wheelbarrows. So, our "earth moving equipment" were gunny sacks with poles running through the sides, making a stretcher like thing. We shoveled dirt onto them and carried them to the strip and dumped it. The idea was to crown the strip in the middle so the water would run off. I don't need to tell you that it took a looooong time to finish the work.

Finally, after months of work we felt that it was ready for inspection. The pilot checked it and approved it.

Repairing Amar airstrip

My experiences growing up in the country really came in handy during that time. We kids would go down to the creek, fill gunny sacks with dirt, and use them along with brush and rocks to dam up the river for a nice swimming pool. So I already knew how to use gunny sacks to haul dirt.

Then it rained, and rained, and rained. Our lovely strip was again a muddy swamp and the pilot again closed it. I won't bore you will all the trying details, but we had four "first landings" and it never was a full load strip, which meant that since it was on sand, we could never get it hard enough for the pilot to take off with a full load. On one occasion, we had been off the station and had an interesting landing when we returned.

This was in my diary during that time:

"Came home yesterday. It had been raining a lot and the airplane stuck in the mud on landing. The village was completely empty as all the people were at the head waters getting food. Mary Owens had come down from Enarotali just to see Amar so we all got out and pushed. We laughed more than we pushed. It took about an hour to get the plane out of the mud."

Airplane stuck in the mud at Amar

"I took off my flip flops to push and forgot to pick them up. When I went back later for them a wild pig had eaten them leaving just a bit as evidence."

Then we came up with an idea, buy a soccer ball and have the men play soccer on the airstrip every afternoon to harden it. That was another of our great ideas that turned out to be one of my biggest challenges at Amar. They were so happy to have a lovely soccer ball. They gathered to play, and after just a few minutes, got into a huge fight. AND they blamed me. They claimed that if f I had not given them the ball, they would not have fought.

Then they decided that if they just had pretty ball shirts they would be so happy. So I bought lovely ball shirts – and they got into a huge fight over them. Naturally it was all my fault for giving them ball shirts.

About that time Marge and I came to the US on furlough and Marge was not able to return to the field. I returned to spend about two years alone there.

This was in my diary during that time when a fight had broken out between the ball teams:

"The Catholic fellows were rude, so Ansel said that our team would quit. They got angry and were beating up on Ansel. I followed the screaming crowd to Napurkama's house. The Catholic teacher commanded God to curse Amar because of the boys who had become Christians, and had left the Catholic Church. Napurukama threatened all of us for our "sins against the government." Then Materaki became very angry and said that we all would be shot. He called several men to come and beat our boys, but they did not come."

"Finally, they all calmed down and shook hands, saying that we would meet the next day to discuss my "forcing" them to change religions. Apparently they have been threatening to beat me up and running me out of the village." I never did understand if the fight was over soccer or the boys changing religions.

Another entry:

"Fine day until Persepeka and Rotak I (names of teams) decided to play ball. All was fine until Rotak made a goal. The people on the side lines began yelling nasty things and making fun of our boys. Willem went off his rocker and went after Augus with a machete. They took it away and he grabbed a stick. They finally cooled down after a full scale Mimika screaming session and went back to the field to shake hands.

"All was well until the chief showed up ranting like a crazy bull. Then he came over screaming at me and I just couldn't take it and came inside. I was pretty upset, and was crying. Nimrod came in to reassure me. Then Wilem came. Then the chief came and apologized. Another normal day at Amar."

I attempted to get the ball players to come and work together to cut the grass on the strip since they were enjoying it. They agreed.

This was in my diary:

"The team *"kesebelasan"* (the eleven) more like *"keti-gaan"* (the three) came and worked. They cut about three blades of grass before collapsing."

The grass had to be cut with machetes and the women would work hard on it and do a good job, but the men were hopeless.

MINISTRY AT AMAR

Catholicism had been there for many years before we came, and breaking through that barrier was next to impossible. The Mimika people also had very little desire to improve their way of life. But God had given me a genuine love for them, and I longed to see them know and love the Lord. A few people did accept Christ, and Ron Hill came and we had our first baptismal service. That night we had our first communion service. It was exciting.

I was working on analyzing the language – making the alphabet, working out the grammar, etc. – and translating a song book, Bible stories, verses, etc. Marge and I both taught Bible Classes while Nimrod Rumpombo started a school and church. Nimrod was a man from the island of Biak and a graduate of our Bible School. He later was martyred for Christ. You will read about him in another chapter.

Nimrod married a Mimika girl and Chuck and Bernita Preston came and Chuck married them. He also married Ansel and a girl who had converted from Catholicism. That exciting wedding is narrated in the chapter on weddings.

KOKONAO LANGUAGE SCHOOL

It was during my time at Amar that I was asked by the Field Council to move back to Kokonao temporarily and teach Indonesian to three new missionaries.

I hired a Muslim soldier to be our language helper. We lost him after three days when I asked him to read Romans 6:23. It was for the students to listen to his pronunciation, and also as a witness to him. An interesting discussion followed his refusal, in which I was informed that I was going to hell. He said that his religion demanded that he kill people like me.

Then he came back. He did agree to read from the New Testament and often stayed after class talking religion. Talking and not listening. He bragged about all the Dutch and communists he had killed and had seen killed. He continued to come and actually began to listen and was obviously interested although he tried hard to disguise it. We became friends. He finally admitted one day that he was a "little bit of a sinner." I told him that if I had to trust in my good works that I would never get to Heaven. He said it was all right, heaven is full enough, so I can keep on believing and not do any good works!

1001 WAYS TO COOK CANNED CORNED BEEF

Supplies were desperately limited during that time and we came up with many ways to cook canned corn beef.

Here is an excerpt from my diary at that time:

"We are all out of meat, vegetables and eggs. Haven't had eggs in weeks. We have eaten canned corned beef until it is about to come out our ears. We had corned beef hash, corned beef in beans, corned beef fried with potatoes, corned beef and potato casserole, corned beef sandwiches, and tomorrow I plan to have a corned beef bread roll."

Also:

"We are still gagging on corned beef. We haven't had eggs in so long that we probably won't recognize them."

This is another excerpt during that time:

"My finances are at their lowest since I became a missionary. Just recalled, though, that I haven't needed a thing."

Recalling the situation then, there was nothing to buy, so we didn't need too much money.

During our time at Amar we sent several of the men to Bible School, and they returned to minister to their own people. Much more could be written about the years I spent at Amar. Marge and I came on furlough together, but she was not able to return due to her parents' illness. I was alone there for about two years. During that time I would go for as many as six weeks without seeing another white person. When the pilot would came with mail and supplies I often begged him to stay for lunch, during which time I would talk his ears off.

After two years alone there in a very difficult place, the mission told me that I would have to move. I moved to Senggo where I spent the next 30 years.

That meant beginning to study my third language - Citak.

Chapter 6

LANGUAGE LEARNING

"Go to, let us go down, and there confound their language, that they may not understand one another's speech." Genesis 11:7

I imagine that every missionary who has ministered in a language different from their own, wishes that the tower of Babel had never happened. How much easier our work would be if we did not have to learn another language.

Before I went to Papua people would sometimes ask me, "What are you going to do on the field?" I knew that they meant was I going to be a teacher, bookkeeper, nurse, etc. The question irritated me. I thought, "I am going to be a missionary. A missionary goes and tells people about Jesus."

However, upon arriving on the field I came very quickly to the rude awakening that I could not tell the people anything. I could not even introduce myself. I could not speak their language. Not only that, I was sure that they were making fun of me. After I began to understand their language I learned they really HAD been making fun of me.

We missionaries desire greatly for the people to whom we minister to "understand" the message of God's love for them. Therefore, learning the language which also includes understanding the culture of the people to whom we minister, is absolutely essential to being an effective missionary.

Language learning can be very rewarding, but can also bring many laughs and a source of real entertainment at the expense of the missionary. At the same time it can be a source of much frustration, discouragement, and humiliation to the "learner." In order to effectively learn a different language one has to be willing to be laughed at and to make an absolute idiot of oneself. I admit that I was good at that.

An entire book could be written on blunders missionaries have made in learning a language different from their own. I certainly made my share of them. We always hope that the ones who heard some of those blunders would have short memories. Most were just funny, while others must be immediately corrected.

I once called a village chief "*kepala*" a coconut "*kelapa*". Once I wanted to invite "*undang*" someone to my home, but said "*udang*" which is "shrimp."

I remember when I was learning Indonesian and my co-worker, Marge Smith, was my teacher. One day some Indonesian soldiers came to the house for some reason. Marge, thinking it would be a wonderful opportunity for me to practice what I had "learned" left the room. I carried on a "conversation" with them which involved them saying something, my understanding a word or two and guessing at the rest, answering what I thought was what the conversation was about, and then repeating the painful dialogue again. Finally, they left. I had no idea what had just happened. Marge's only comment was, "You were carrying on two different conversations." That was in the Indonesian language which is considered to be a fairly easy language to learn.

MIMIKA AND CITAK LANGUAGES

Then came the tribal language Mimika and later, Citak. That was a completely different situation since neither of those languages had ever been written and no outsider had ever learned them. So how does one go about learning a language that has never been written? It stands to reason that someone must write it. In the next chapter you will read about that experience.

Oftentimes overcoming the language barrier does not just mean that you can speak, and hopefully, be understood. You must also learn how they communicate. They often take it for granted that you understand them even when they do not use enough words to make themselves clear. Perhaps they think that the fewer words they use the more likely it will be that we will understand. Asking the right questions also helps.

"WHERE IS THE SICK BABY?"

Ruth was the nurse. I was at her house one day when a man came in a panic. Ruth could not understand all that he said, but understood "baby" and "sick" so she figured that there was a sick baby somewhere. She asked how long it had been sick, "Since this morning," he replied. Ruth asked why he hadn't brought the baby with him and he just stared at her obviously worried. She asked where the baby was and he still just stared at her. She kept asking things like, "Is it at the hospital? Is it in the village?" He wouldn't say a word.

Finally, I decided that I would try my hand at trying to figure him out. I went out and asked again where the baby was and he replied, "Stomach." By that time I guess he knew that we would not understand complete sentences.

I decided that the baby was sick in the stomach – wherever it was! So I asked again where the baby was.

"Nona, it hasn't been born yet!" he replied. His wife was in labor at the hospital, and he needed the nurse quick! We all had a good laugh, and the nervous father-to-be even laughed a bit.

"HELP HER UNDERSTAND, LORD"

You will read later about my first and best friend at Senggo, Pemar Bagasu. She would patiently bear with me while I tried to communicate. One day she prayed, "Lord, I come here every day and tell her the names of all the fish, birds, trees, and snakes, and she still doesn't understand. Help her to understand." AMEN!

I would work with the helpers in the morning and then go and sit in the village in the afternoon and "talk" with the ladies. Sometimes, they would be intimidated and would not say a word.

One afternoon I came up with a bright idea. We were all sitting on the floor, so I would just lie down on the floor and pretend to be asleep. Then they would talk among themselves while I listened. That turned out to be a bad idea. One of the ladies said, "Be quiet, she is asleep." They all joined me on the floor and went to sleep!

"WHAT'S WRONG WITH HER MOUTH HOLE?"

They were used to me writing the words in my notebook. One day Ruth and I were visiting in the village and Ruth was practicing the pronunciation of a particularly difficult word. She kept asking Pemar to repeat it and then she would attempt to mimic her. Finally, Pemar turned to me and said, "Tell her to write it in her book."

I said, "She has it written in her book, but she can't make it come out of her mouth correctly."

About that time Pemar's little boy, Andreas, came in an observed a while and then said to Pemar, "Tell her to write it in her book." Pemar said, "She has written it in her book, but can't make it come out of her mouth correctly." Looking intently at Ruth's mouth, he asked, "What is wrong with her mouth hole?" Yeah, we too wanted to know that. We often had trouble with our mouth holes.

CURSING IN CITAK

Like people everywhere, the Citak people loved a good joke. They have a lovely sense of humor, and sometimes they would crack up with laughter over something that I failed to see what was so funny. I would in turn tell them something that I thought was really funny, and they would just stare at me obviously not seeing anything funny about it.

I would study with my language helpers all morning and then visit in the village in the afternoon. I knew only a few Citak words at the time. The ladies would tell me things which I promptly wrote in my book, having no idea what they were. I did not know enough Citak to ask questions.

One afternoon the ladies all gathered around for my afternoon "language lesson." Pemar and gang gave me a word I had never heard. I wrote it in my book. Then I repeated it. They howled with laughter. Assuming that I must have heard them wrong, I had them say it again. I was thinking, "I have written it exactly the way they are saying it." So, I repeated it again. They again howled with laughter. After several attempts, I figured that I would just pass on that one and get another word. They gave me another word. I wrote it down and repeated it to them. They laughed even harder than they had at the first word.

I left it for another word, and the same process was repeated by me saying the word over and over again trying to get it right, while they were almost in tears from laughter. This went on all afternoon, and I had a whole page of words that were causing me no end of frustration, thinking that I must be missing something important, since I could not get the pronunciation right.

The next morning I told Abdon, who understood a bit of Indonesian, "Listen to these words, tell me the meanings and tell me what I am doing wrong." I repeated the first word. Abdon's eyes got big. I repeated several more of the words. Abdon's eyes got bigger. "Where did you get those words?" he asked.

It turned out that the lovely ladies had had a wonderfully entertaining afternoon at my expense teaching me dozens of dirty words which I had repeated over and over again. At least after that I knew when the people were calling each other bad names!

DID JESUS REALLY HAVE A TAIL?

The Citak people had no problem believing in the resurrection of Christ. After all, they "saw" the spirits of their departed loved ones quite frequently. One day in my early days at Senggo, I learned by accident that they did not believe in the bodily resurrection of Jesus. That must be corrected, I thought. I studied very hard wanting to be sure to get this one right.

Then came the big day when I was going to set the record straight. Pat, a fellow missionary, was in the ladies' class when I first taught the lesson. I felt that I had been presenting it clearly. Then I came to the all-important punch line. What I meant to say was, "A spirit does not have flesh and bones as I do." As soon as I delivered that statement, Pat began frantically waving her arms. I had no idea what she was so excited about. The women just sat there with straight faces like, "If you say so, it must be correct." What I had said was, "A spirit does not have flesh and a tail as I do." The difference was "bone" (*emak*), and "tail" (*epmak*). What a difference one letter makes.

After many months and even years, we finally found ourselves able to communicate. I remember sitting on the floor with a group of people in one of the village houses. We were all laughing, talking, and exchanging stories. I realized that I was joining in, understanding, and being understood. What a thrill!

All the frustration and hard work of language study is forgotten when we can explain the love of God in their language, and see the light in their eyes when they understand.

Language learning though, had to be accompanied by the task of analyzing and writing the language as well.

Chapter 7

LANGUAGE ANALYSIS

Perhaps the most rewarding part of my ministry in Papua was the indescribable joy and responsibility of translating the New Testament into two tribal languages – Citak and Asmat/Tamnim. Neither of those languages had been written and it was fun – most of the time – reducing these languages to writing. That involved, first of all, training helpers to work with me.

They had never had to get used to fitting into any kind of schedule, so one of my first and biggest challenges was to train them to come to work every day, and to come on time! If it rained, I could forget having anyone come, because rain stopped literally everything. If they were asked why they did not come to work when they were supposed to, the simple answer was, "It rained." No other explanation was needed.

Titus Fiak was one of my first helpers. You will read more about this man who was used mightily by God in the ministry of language analysis and Bible translation. The helpers could come up with many creative excuses for not coming to work. One day Titus did not show up for work. That afternoon I went down to the village to check on him. I was informed that he had been out in the jungle working on his canoe all day. The next morning I was in the middle of a very stern lecture about how working on his canoe was definitely NOT, in my opinion, an excuse for not coming to work. He, not so nicely, interrupted me by saying, "Nona, I had diarrhea, and if I am out in the jungle working on my canoe, I am right there where I can go. If I am here working with you, I can't go." I felt it was time to interrupt him before he gave more details than I wanted, and quickly excused him for not coming to work.

It is one of the joys of the ministry when the people understand your jokes. On the other hand, it is a great accomplishment if you ever get to the point that you understand *their* humor. Another time when Titus had not come to work, and there were many days when he did not, I went again to the village to check on him. The people told me that he was out fishing. I jokingly declared that I was going to beat him when he returned. Just as I said that he appeared, coming down the path toward the village with his bow and arrows, spear, fish line, etc.

Let me explain how the Citak people fight. They get out in the middle of the village with their spears, and bows and arrows and yell, calling out threats and ugly names. They will pull back on the bow strings making a loud twang. Hardly anyone ever gets hurt but they sure make a lot of noise. If they do actually fight and someone bleeds, the one who causes the blood is automatically at fault. He must make restitution regardless of what the fight was about.

When Titus appeared the people laughingly said, "There he comes now. Beat him up." I grabbed a spear lying near the house and ran out into the middle of the village brandishing it. Although he had not heard our conversation, Titus caught on immediately. He threw down all the things he had in his hand except for his bow and we had a huge "fight" in the middle of the village, to the delight of the villagers. I love Titus!

Then there was Abdon. I often called him "Petrus" (Peter) because he always had something to say. I loved his giggle. When I first went to Senggo, Abdon worked with me on the language. He was not yet married. However, he was desperately in love with Naomi. Marriages were normally arranged by the families involved, and sometimes they were even forced. Not so with Abdon and Naomi. She was working in our mission hospital and had to pass right by where I was living. I would be engrossed in the language and without any warning would completely lose Abdon. He heard nothing that I said and it was impossible to get his attention. His eyes and mind were glued on Naomi walking past on her way to work, and all I could do was to sit and wait.

They got married and had several children. I never knew them to have a fight except one time after several years of marriage. Abdon got malaria and was very sick for several days. The Citak men would often shave their heads when they were sick. They said their hair was too heavy! Abdon had shaved his head.

He was feeling much better, and Naomi wanted to go into the jungle with the other ladies to gather food. He wanted her to stay home and take care of him. Naomi went anyway. They had a really big fight in the middle of the village. They were calling each other dirty names which I cannot repeat. But what really offended Abdon was when she called him "bald head."

He came marching to my house and wanted Ruth and I to go to the village immediately and let Naomi know that he was the boss, and that she was supposed to obey him. God made them that way! He said he was going to "throw her away." We talked with both of them, and I reminded Abdon about how much in love he was, and teased him about seeing nothing but her when she passed by. He began his giggle and they were fine, and I never knew them to fight openly again.

God used wonderful men like Titus and Abdon, as well as others whom you will read about in another chapter to help create the written language, and translate the New Testament. It never would have been accomplished without them. God took uneducated, primitive men, saved them, filled them with His Spirit, and used them mightily to help translate His Word into their language.

That should serve as a reminder to us. God does not choose us because we are worthy or that we somehow think we are qualified. He chooses whom He wants, and then supplies what we need to do His will.

Let me get back to telling you about language analysis. First, I had to develop an alphabet. That involved getting several hundred words and writing them phonetically as they sound using the International Phonetic Alphabet. I won't bore you with the process, but "phonetic" sounds were converted to "phonemic" ones where pronunciation rules were made, and as many as possible of the consonants and vowels were dropped.

Years were spent figuring out their grammar and writing the rules. That process is fun if you enjoy working puzzles as it involved finding the symmetry in their language and describing it. I began that work before the age of computers, which made it more painstaking since everything had to be written by hand. Then came the task of making a dictionary.

All of the work was done with these goals in mind: learn to communicate in Citak, explain God's love to them, and translate God's Word.

Chapter 8

LITERACY

There was no need to translate if nobody could read what was translated. Literacy was not my forte, and I had to have help from my former co-worker, Marge Smith, a former school teacher, in making the primers. I found that making primers was the easy part. Teaching them was something else.

It was 1977 when my first literacy course got started off with a bang. After spending many hours making the first Citak Primers and building up enthusiasm among the Citak people, I announced the first class. The women were embarrassed to come to class with the men, so I had to have two classes daily, one for the women and one for the men.

After a couple of days, the women took their books home, proudly clutching their pretty yellow books which they still did not know how to hold right side up. When Pemar arrived home with her book, her husband, Turbis, became very angry because he "was embarrassed that she would bring a book home when she couldn't read." He beat her badly, almost breaking her arm, and somehow managed to stab a stick all the way through her finger and burned her precious book. You may read more about this lovely man in the chapter titled, "People I Can't Forget".

When the ladies came to class the next day it was obvious that they had not done their homework. They had taken their books home and had hidden them, "So people wouldn't laugh at us," they said. Eventually they did become proud of their books and would openly "read" them together in the village.

We believed that in order for the Citak people to grow spiritually, they must have Scripture in their own language and, of course, must be able to read it. Unfortunately, I did not shine as a literacy teacher.

The students were mostly adults or older children, and the first big problem was to teach them how to hold a pencil. Also I tried to make them understand that if they didn't talk and laugh so much they could learn quicker. They had never had to do the same thing every day such as attend a class, so if they did not feel like it, they just didn't come. They would go into the jungle for food for days at a time. Some days everybody would be in class, other days only two or three, and sometimes no one would show up. It's not that they were not interested. They were interested – that is just how they live.

Their method of learning was by watching someone else do it and mimicking them. They had never learned to analyze or figure things out, and that made for some interesting and VERY frustrating classes. They were good at memorizing, and had memorized all the syllables. Then came what I had expected to be an exciting time. I very proudly announced, "We can put these syllables together and they will make words, then you will be able to read!"

I held up the syllable "KA". They all said, "KA". Then I held up the syllable "KI". They read it. Then I held up both of them together and asked, "Now what is the word?" They looked and looked for quite a while and finally someone said, "tame?" I will spare you the rest of the story, but literacy was an extremely frustrating experience for me. I also learned very early not to tell someone that they had made a mistake. It resulted in them being so intimidated that neither that lady nor any other lady would say another word for the rest of the class.

They had a very complicated language, which added to the struggles in learning to read it. For example, "See Jane run," is translated as, "*Jane zenak batatina banak bapurabure.*" That is, if Jane were running between about 10 a.m. and 3 p.m., and if she were running the direction away from the large river. If she were running before about 10 a.m. it would be, "*Jane zenak batatinita banak bapuritabure.*" If she were running between about 3 p.m. and dark it would be, "*Jane zenak batatinasima banak bapurasimabure.*" If she ran after dark and before daylight it would be, "*Jane zenak batatinasa banak bapurasabure.*" If that didn't confuse you enough, it changed if Jane were running another direction depending on the relationship to the large river. It amazed me that anyone could learn to read.

Some of them did learn to read, but not without sometimes wishing they had not.

THE JOYS OF LETTER WRITING

One of the most frustrating experiences I had with house/yard help was with them learning to write. Timo was afraid to come right out and ask me for an advance on his salary, which was an almost daily occurrence. He knew that I would fuss at him, so he feared to ask for it. He would work all day, go home, and then send a note back to me by a small boy. That was irritating.

Also irritating was that he didn't have enough writing skills to make it clear just what he wanted. Once he asked for Rp.500, which was about a nickel. Although I knew that he wanted much more, I sent him just what he asked for. It took only a few minutes for him to show up at my front door, explaining to me what he really wanted. I told him that I sent just what he asked for. The next time that happened he asked for Rp.500,000,000,000. I guess he figured that I would erase the extra 0's.

One trick the Citak people were fond of using was to try to shame the missionaries into giving them what they wanted. They did this by writing letters asking for what they wanted and ending with something like, "If you really love me, you will give it to me." When that hardly ever worked they would write, "If you really are a Christian, you will give it to me." No one who ever wrote that got what they were asking for from me.

Sometimes I thought, "Whose idea was it to teach these people to read and write?" As they learned to read, I translated other material. First was a song book, which they loved. Several of the missionaries contributed to the songs for the song books, which were revised several times. I also translated a Bible Study Course. The "readers" would read it and answer the questions and receive awards.

Since only a few people could read at that time, we invited Gospel Recordings missionaries to come and record the lessons on tapes. We had tape players that ran without batteries, by winding them, which we distributed to the outlying villages. They were supposed to be "native proof." They weren't. I found myself spending lots of time trying to repair broken tape players. They learned to open them using a nail as a screw driver and parts would be missing. They always said, "I didn't open it."

By that time we had opened a school, and the children were learning to read in Indonesian. That was not the best solution, as they understood little or no Indonesian at the time, but did help them to learn to read. Now that they can read, things can really progress. We learned that reading also presented its challenges.

Chapter 9

CITAK WORLD VIEW

O ne would think, "Now that the language has been written down, I have learned to communicate a bit, some of the people have learned to read, some material has been translated, things are ready to roll." So I thought. I had begun to teach Bible stories to the people, which they loved hearing. I had prepared to teach the story about the wide road that leads to destruction, and the narrow road that leads to life everlasting using a large picture roll to illustrate the story.

As I was telling the story the people became really excited. Sahu said, "Nona, everybody needs to hear that! Can we take the picture roll and go to all the outlying villages and tell that to everybody?" I was pleased at their reaction, but wondered why after all the stories I had told them they were excited about that particular one. You will understand that shortly.

It was around that time we felt that we needed to do an in-depth study about the Citak World View. We needed to know what they believed. Where did they come from? What were their beliefs concerning the spirits? What did they believe concerning the afterlife? What are their customs?

We needed the answers to these very important questions if we were to teach them effectively, and if we were to correctly translate the Scriptures. Knowing some of these things also protects the missionary from making big mistakes that could deeply offend the people. This study took several years and even then I could not say that it had been completed.

At first they were reluctant to share some of their "secrets" with an outsider. In time they gradually began to trust me. I remember one of the first ones to open up to me. He was a witch doctor named Zuam. He would come and sit for hours telling legends and answering questions. Later, his son Timo worked for me for many years. Others also began to open up and I was able to record and study dozens of legends from both men and women. The result of that study was written mainly for the use of the other missionaries, and was invaluable in understanding the people I had come to love.

Here is just a bit of that study. The complete Citak World View may be obtained by contacting me.

BODY LANGUAGE

Learning their spoken language was important. Learning their body language was also important. The body gestures that they used most often, included raising the eyebrows to indicate an affirmative answer, slapping the chest to indicate excitement or surprise, slapping under the arm to indicate something very far away, and pointing with the lower lip.

They count by using their fingers and toes. They begin with the thumb on one hand, go to the other hand, then to the big toe on one foot, and then to the other foot. Once that was done, if they needed to count further, they would put one person aside, which signified the number 20, and then begin counting another set of fingers and toes. Teaching about the feeding of the 5000 that way could have been very interesting.

I learned that one gesture was very useful and indeed necessary to know. When we as Americans say, "There is one God," we normally gesture by holding up our index finger. If I did that in Citak, I was saying "one" but showing "two". In Citak, "one" is shown by holding up the thumb. "Two" is the thumb and index finger, which is what they see when we hold up the index finger.

BELIEFS IN THE SUPERNATURAL

The Citak people believed in a variety of supernatural beings, as well as certain humans, "witch doctors", who were either empowered by the spirits, or who had the power to turn themselves temporarily into a spirit. The spirits had the power to cause sickness or death.

A. Spirits
1. Tree Top Spirits – *"bu"*
The tree top spirits, referred to as *"usu busur bu"*, are spirits who live in the atmosphere over the tree tops. They have always existed. There are a lot of interesting legends about these spirits.

The chief of these spirits, who was the first one, was Daru. They have no family name for these spirits. Daru's wife was Tawa. They had two sons, Dasawu, the oldest, and Börbit.

Dasawu had very black skin and had two wives. They both had the same name – Tansiraut. They also had black skin. Dasawu was ugly and deformed. His legs were crooked. He was skinny, had tangled hair, a wide nose, and couldn't talk plain. He was mischievous and enjoyed playing tricks on Börbit.

Börbit had three wives, whose names were all the same, Taraut. Börbit and his wives were all light skinned and beautiful. Börbit enjoyed hunting.

Dasawu and Börbit are generally given credit for being the originator of most things. One legend teller, Pumak, had heard the teachings about God and creation. One day when she was telling legends to me, I wanted to see how she was processing the teachings about God. "Who created everything?" I asked. She thought for a while obviously trying to make sense out of things, and finally answered, "Probably God created Dasawu and then Dasawu created people."

The *"bu"* spirits live much like people. They live in houses, have children, go hunting, and eat pork, grubs, sago. etc.

These are the most powerful of the spirits, but less feared. They are immoral, but are considered to be basically good, although they are capable of doing bad things. When the people use magic to get pigs, etc., they expect the help to come from these spirits. These spirits do kill people in order to help them. For example, if a man has two wives, and he isn't nice to one of them, these spirits may feel sorry for her and kill her, so they can care for her themselves. People cannot go to the tree tops when they die.

People are these spirits before they are born. While the mother is pregnant and before they are born, they come in the form of the *"zibir"* (spirit of living people), and meet the *"zibir"* of the witch doctor from their clan in the jungle, and give him their name and also give some taboos for the mother. This usually is some food such as fish, grubs, sago, etc., which she may not eat, or some activity such as paddling a canoe, which she may not do during the pregnancy and infancy. If she breaks the taboo, either she or the baby will die. She may eat the taboo food when the baby himself gets big enough to pick it up and eat it himself. Also, she may resume the activity when the baby does it.

This was important for the medical staff as well and the rest of us to understand and to deal with. Before understanding this, I remember trying hard to get a sick pregnant lady to eat some fish that I felt that she needed to eat. She would clinch her teeth shut and refuse it. Understanding their fear of the taboos helped us keep from costly cultural blunders and to be able to teach them from God's Word.

2. Dreams and the shadow/spirit of living people – *"zibir"*

The person's *"zibir"* can leave his body during sleep and go out and do things which are revealed to the person through dreams. The *"zibir"* also leaves the body during serious illness, but can be brought back sometimes by the witch doctor's *"zibir"*. The *"zibir"* leaves the body at death and becomes a *"büü"*. The *"zibir"* cannot be seen by humans. It can be seen and talked to by another *"zibir"*.

The Citak people believe that what they see in most, but not all of their dreams, is actually the *"zibir"* of the person they dream about. They fear their dreams and feel that what they dream has actually happened or will happen. They seldom would say, "I dreamed that So-and-So put a curse on me and said that I would die in three days." But they would say, "So-and-So put a curse on me and I will die in three days." And they do, indeed, die in three days. If a lady dreams that a man asked her to have an affair with him, her husband will fight the man whom she dreamed about just as if he had actually come to her.

If a person dreams something bad about a friend, that curse can be removed by going through a ritual. The person who dreamed would go to the one whom he dreamed about and report the dream to him. If that person wants to remove the curse, then he will wipe his underarm perspiration on the one who dreamed, and then that one will crawl three times between the legs of the one he dreamed about.

We had to learn not to scoff at their deep beliefs in dreams, but to deal gently as we taught them.

3. Jungle spirits and spirits who live under the ground – *"büü"*

"Büü" is a general word for all the spirits who live on the earth or under the ground. They are also sometimes referred to as *"zuma"*. The ones who live in the jungle, *"wasan büü"* and the ones who live under the ground *"se zipa aman büü"* are about the same.

There are also *"büü"* who live in the *"etua"* (banyan) tree.

The *"wasan büü"* live in a village up above the Brazza area (western Citak). When we began to visit in that area in the early 1980's, the Senggo people were afraid for us to go there.

There are *"büü"* who existed before the world, and others are the spirits of dead people. When a person dies, his *"zibir"* leaves him and becomes a *"büü"*. The *"büü"* goes to the *"büü"* village where they test him by giving him food. If he eats it all himself and does not share it, then they show him a large path which leads to the middle of the village. They deceive him into going down that path where he falls into a large hole that they have set as a trap where he is closed up and can never come out again.

I see a real inconsistency here as the people say that they see the *"büü"* and they come and make noises in their houses to frighten them, but nobody seems to have the answer as to how they do that if they are in the hole in the ground. When they say that they never come out of the ground again, they may mean that they never come out as the *"zibir"* or in bodily form.

If the *"büü"* divides the food given to him, then he is shown a small path that leads into the village where he is welcomed by his ancestors and lives there. Neither of these places is a desirable place. They eat roundworms, centipedes, dirt, decayed wood, and feces.

It was this belief about the two paths that had caused the big reaction to the story about the two roads. I will deal more with this in the next chapter.

When we first entered the Brazza area village of Vakabüis, they had never seen a white person and thought I was a *"büü"*. Then I confirmed it by opening my thermos and drinking coffee which they thought was fecal water! That took away my appetite for coffee for a long time.

The *"büü"* are bad spirits and are the ones that are greatly feared by the people, and are usually synonymous with Satan. Because of the sensitive nature of some of these beliefs, I will leave out much of it.

The *"büü"* can take on the form of a husband or wife, so when people go to the jungle the man keeps looking back to be sure his wife does not get out of sight so he can be sure she is really his wife.

The *"büü"* can "slap" people and cause them to be suddenly deaf. They kill people by shooting them with a short arrow in one of the places of death, which are the upper stomach, left ribs, back of the neck, throat, and the back of the jaw. The arrow cannot be seen as it is short and goes all the way in. The *"aurat ibit"* (witch doctor) may sometimes pull this out.

The *"büü"* kill people they are angry with, or people they want for themselves. I never found out what would make a *"büü"* angry. My informants say that in the old days, if someone stole a lot, lied, or generally caused trouble in the village, the people themselves would use magic, *"swa puka"*, so the *"büü"* would kill him so the rest of the village could live in peace.

B. Practitioners (Witch doctors)

1. *"Aurat kaü"*

"Aurat kaü" can only be males. The *"aurat kaü"* are mainly known for their ability to turn themselves into some kind of animal – usually a snake or wild boar. They are powerful and feared by the people. Their *"zibir"* goes out of the body while the *"aurat kaü"* are sleeping and turns into an animal. Then if someone who is out hunting in the jungle shoots that animal, it gives the *"aurat kaü"* an excuse to kill him. When the hunter returns to the village, the *"aurat kaü"* wakes up, tells who killed him, and the hunter dies.

The *"zibir"* of the *"aurat kaü"* can go into the *"büü"* village under the ground and get diseases to make people sick or die. People may seek the help of the *"aurat kaü"* to get revenge on their enemy. The people pay him for his services. The *"aurat kaü"* will either turn into an animal and "slap" the person when he is out in the jungle, or will cause him to be very sick. Once a person has been "slapped" by the curse, there is nothing he can do about it unless the *"aurat kaü"* themselves remove the curse. Nobody that I have talked with believes that the *"aurat kaü"* would remove the curse.

The *"aurat kaü"* give the names of the unborn baby to the expectant mother, as well as taboos for her to follow.

They can make people well by pulling out the offending thing from the body, such as a termite, red ant, dry leaf, arrow point, cassowary claw, pig tusk, etc. It is removed by massaging the body while chanting, to bring it to the surface, and then pulling it out with his teeth. Then they show it to the people.

They can also turn themselves into a year bird which pulls things out of people's stomachs to make them well.

They are able to tell who caused another person to be sick or die.

2. *"Bu kaü"*

"Bu kaü" do many of the same things the *"aurat kaü"* do. Both males and females can be *"bu kaü"*. Whereas the *"aurat kaü"* go into the ground and get power from the *"büü"*, the *"bu kaü"*, in the form of their *"zibir"*, can climb vines up above the trees and commune with the *"bu"*. They are more benevolent than the *"aurat kaü"*. They can also turn themselves into animals, put curses on people to make them sick or die, name unborn babies, and give taboos to the pregnant women. They also heal people, but they are not able to show what they pull out of sick individuals.

People pay the *"bu kaü"* to do incantations to help them to be successful when they go hunting.

3. Magic – *"swa puka"*

This is the most widely used magic. Things used are the leaves or bark of certain trees – *"piri etan"*, *"pasi etan"*, *"kwar etan"*, *"puru fase"*, *"umu fase"*, and *"amun fase"*. Anybody who learns the incantations can use this, and as far as I can tell, everybody knows at least some of the incantations. The person says the chant into the leaf or bark and puts it near the front door at night. The person walks over it and the curse is on him and he will either become sick or die.

There are many kinds of *"swa"*. It can be used to get pigs in the jungle by putting the bark on the bow to attract the pigs. It is also put in pig traps. Offended wives use to make their husbands' scrotum swell. It is also used to make people skinny, etc.

Certain women can use this to help barren women become pregnant. However, it has its drawbacks as it can't be reversed, and the girl faces the problem of having more pregnancies than she wanted.

C. Cause of Sickness and Death

Sickness must have a cause, and the only logical cause the Citak people can come up with is magic in the form of *"swa"* or caused by the *"aurat"* or *"bu kaü"*. When someone would die they would always blame someone – the wife or husband were the first ones to be blamed.

As they are learning more about medicine and the scientific causes of certain sickness, they openly accept the explanations given by the medical people, but in practice it is obvious that many of the people still hold on to their old beliefs.

D. Protective Measures

Protective measures against sickness or death include avoiding the breaking of taboos, resolving conflicts with enemies, and ritual performances as in the case of dreams. The *"aurat kaü"* and *"bu kaü"* can be called to heal, or *"swa puka"* can be used.

As the Citak people began to understand more about disease and their cause, and *"aurat kau"* began to die out. However, the *"bu kau"* remained a powerful force.

Again, because of the delicate nature of some explanations, I will omit most of their beliefs concerning pregnancy and child birth. I include just a summary here.

They have beliefs about how a lady becomes pregnant, and what can be done to prevent it. Also, the reason for barrenness and how it can be overcome.

A fetus is a *"bu"*. Miscarriages are believed to be caused by the *"bu"* or *"büü"*. They have beliefs about stillbirth.

Babies born with major birth defects are not recognized as being human, but are still the *"bu"*, and therefore are killed at birth.

The people often married cousins and I often wondered why we did not see more physical or mental defects. Learning this helped to understand.

E. Twins

The people in most of the villages do keep twins now, but they used to believe that the second child was conceived by a "*bu*" or "*büü*".

Others believe that the mother had eaten two fruits growing together, layers of sago. Etc.

It took a long time and much patience in teaching them about twins. They feared to keep the twins. I wondered how they knew which one to kill, and was told that they killed the smallest one. Most of the time, they would put one stick behind the baby's neck and one in front and squeeze them until the baby died. Other times, they would just not feed the baby and it would die from starvation. The husband would also beat his wife.

Sometimes the hospital staff would ask me to come and talk to the parents when twins had been born. I would, first of all, talk with the husband and encourage him not to beat his wife. I would then speak with the mother. They would promise not to kill one of the babies, and then almost immediately go into the jungle for several days. When they returned, they only had one baby. They would merely say, "It died."

We tried about everything. We taught them from the medical point of view, that the babies were wonderful gifts from God, and that the spirits had nothing to do with it. They continued to kill the twin.

Then Noak Fiak was ministering in the village of Komasma. A lady had twins and they had buried one of them alive. Noak ran out and dug the baby out of the dirt and took it home. The people begged him not to keep it and assured him that he and/or the baby would die. Noak and Paulina kept the baby and he grew up into a healthy young man. He is married with children of his own now.

The people watched to see if Noak or the baby would die. When they did not even get sick, it became the breakthrough that we needed. We had felt that if just one person would keep the twins, then others would be encouraged to keep them.

Now when they have twins, they seem so proud of them. Bidaw was from Vakabuis. One day we went there for a visit and Bidaw came out all excited and exclaimed, "My wife had twins! We did not kill our twin!" Those were the first twins to survive in Vakabuis.

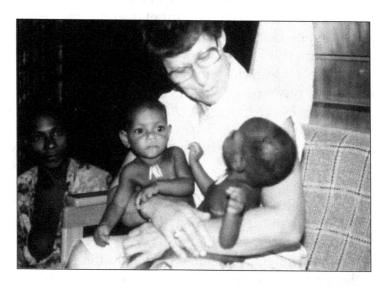

Vakabuis twins

If the mother eats certain fish, including *"biri"* and *"amu"* they believe that the baby will not develop well and may be crippled or have lots of sores.

Eating snakes, or animal tails are believed to keep the placenta from delivering.

F. Death

When a man is very sick and it is felt that he is dying, the oldest daughter's husband must sit cross legged on the floor holding the dying person's head on his lap. (If a woman dies, then the oldest son's wife does that.) He continues to hold it during the time of mourning after the person dies. That would usually be for several hours. The in-laws must stay with the body and protect the family from hurting themselves while they mourn, roll in the mud, etc. The in-laws also bathe the body and take it to the grave. The oldest daughter's husband carries the head. Anyone outside the family may help dig the grave.

This was really helpful for me to understand. The temptation was to be very close to them during the mourning time. I wanted to take a turn holding the person's head, or help bathe the body, etc. Understanding this culture was valuable in knowing what to do and perhaps even more, knowing what not to do.

The wife of a dead man may not go out fishing or to process sago, nor may she eat until her husband's family offer her food and invite her to go out to get food. The length of time for this depends on how they viewed her care for her husband. She may be given food to eat within 2-3 days, but may have to wait as long as a month before going out to hunt for food.

Before I knew this custom, I tried very hard to get a grieving wife to eat. She had not eaten in about three days and I was concerned for her. She clinched her teeth together and refused. It turned out that her in-laws were angry at her and blamed her for her husband's death.

G. Miscellaneous Beliefs

It is bad luck to walk directly behind a person or to step in their footprints.

It is bad luck to eat pig and fish in the same day. Also sago grubs and cuscus.

If one eats *"tawer"* (large wood grub) and hear of the "pisi" palm together he will be struck by lightning.

If you scrape pig tusk and cook it with sago and feed it to a person, he will be bitten by a pig.

If a mother eats mushrooms she will not have milk for her baby.

I cannot overemphasize the importance of missionaries understanding the customs and culture of the people they want to love and win to the Lord. In the next chapter I will give some of their beliefs concerning the origin of various things.

Chapter 10

ORIGIN LEGENDS/MYTHS

The complete paper about the study I did concerning their origin and historical legends may be obtained by requesting it from me. Here I will only include some of the more interesting legends about the origin of various things.

A. Earthquakes

The people were out staying where they could get sago grubs. A man named Ayö went off the path to have a bowel movement. On his way back, he slipped and fell down sideways into the mud and couldn't get up. Every time he would twist or try to turn to get up, the ground would shake. His grandson tied poles to him so he wouldn't move, and gave him some of the grubs and left him. He would come back and check on him, but could not get him out of the mud because the ground would shake so badly. That was the beginning of earthquakes.

The Citak word for "earthquake" is *"ayö."* They believe that when there are earth tremors, it is the man trying to get up. If he succeeds in getting up the end of the world will come. During an earthquake or earth tremors, they will often run outside and shoot and ground with their bows and arrows trying to kill Ayö and to keep him from getting up.

B. Moon

Some people were in the jungle having a picnic. They had a head that they had taken in war. They wove a small basket and put the head in it and left it with the old people to guard while they went into the jungle to hunt for food. While they were gone, a lady came and said, "What is this? Did you make this?" She looked inside the basket and was about to pick up the head, when it when it came flying out of the basket, and flew up into the fronds of a palm tree.

The people returned and began to cut the palm tree down, but when it started to fall, the head went flying out of it and hung in the sky down river (west). When it got dark, it opened its eyes, and became the moon. It told the sun, "I will come out at night, and when I sink into the water down river, I will make you come up."

C. Fire

In the beginning, the people did not have fire. They would eat their sago grubs, and sago, raw. Then one day a bird of paradise woman came and said, "You are eating the food raw. Don't you have a fire?" The people said, "No." She flew away and got a fire and gave it to the people, so they all have fire now.

D. Fish

In the beginning, the fish were people. Börbit would go to the fish people village, and eat sago grubs with them, and spend the night there. Once Dasawu followed his footprints to the fish people's village. They gave him sago grubs, and he went to sleep. When he slept, the people put their skins on the rack to go in the water, and they rattled and woke up Dasawu. He pretended to be asleep, so the fish people went into the water.

While they were swimming, Dasawu ate all their skins and then went back to sleep. In the morning, when they wanted to come back on the shore, they couldn't because he had eaten their skins, so they stayed in the water and became fish.

E. Water Snakes

People were seining for fish when they heard some birds squawking at a snake in the top of a tree. They cut down the tree and killed the snake. They thought that there was something taboo about the snake, so they cut it open from head to tail leaving the skin, but taking out the stomach. They left it and went to sleep. During the night, the intestines slid down into the water and became all kinds of water snakes.

F. Canoes

One of the water snakes came wiggling back and forth up the river. It had turned into a canoe and came like it had a motor on it. The man tried to get in it, but it went away very quickly and disappeared down river, turned around and came back again.

G. Dogs

Pigs apparently made dogs. However, the pigs and dogs began to attack each other. When the animal with a bushy tail ran out, the people said, "This must be a dog." They took it and raised it and dogs multiplied from it.

There was just one man in the village, and when the dogs multiplied, he gave them out to the other villages, and told them that if they raised the dogs they would multiply.

H. Rainbows

The first people cut off an enemy's head and wrapped his gall bladder around a pole and it turned into a rainbow. When it was night it went and hung in the sky.

The Citak word for "gallbladder" is *"ziri"*, and "rainbow" is *"pituziri"*. I asked them why they didn't just call it *"ziri"* and they said so they would not think it was a gallbladder!

Conclusion

One of the biggest challenges in studying the legends of the Citak people was to try to make them sound consistent, or to make them sensible. I did not succeed! When I would point out an inconsistency to them they would just look at me as if to say, "You don't try to make sense out them, you just listen to them."

However, I learned a lot about how the Citak people though, and how they saw themselves. This was all VERY helpful in the big task of translating the New Testament into their language.

Chapter 11

REDEMPTIVE ANALOGIES

D on Richardson wrote in two of his books, *"Peace Child,"* and *"Eternity In Their Hearts,"* very interesting illustrations of what he calls "redemptive analogies." I highly recommend both of these books.

As he so effectively taught, God in His infinite wisdom and love has put things into primitive cultures, which we as missionaries can find, and use to point them to Him. He calls those "redemptive analogies."

You have already read about the narrow road and the wide road. As soon as I learned about their beliefs we were able to capitalize on that and use it to teach them. We had the story in Scripture about the two roads.

I asked around, trying to learn who they thought had gone into the village after death and not the hole in the ground. They answered that nobody had ever gone to that village.

"Why?" I asked. "Because everybody had done wrong and did not share their food," they replied.

What an opportunity to tell them that God has a really nice village – nothing like the village they talked about. In God's village, nobody fights, no one gets killed, no one gets hungry, no one gets sick, no one cries, and no one dies.

There indeed are two paths and the wide path leads to hell – under the ground. The narrow one leads to God's village in the sky.

Yes, everyone has done wrong. Nobody has ever lived a perfect life. Yet God loves us and wants every one of us to go to His village, so He opened a path for us. Then we taught them about how God sent Jesus, who never sinned and died to abolish our sins so that we could go to His village.

One day a Christian man died and I went down to the village to be with the people. They were mourning, wailing, and rolling in the mud as was their custom. The man's daughter, who was about 12 years old, was crying, and as tears rolled down her little cheeks she kept saying something over and over again. I moved closer in order to hear what she was saying. "My daddy is in the hole in the ground. My daddy is in the hole in the ground," she repeated over and over.

I put my arm around her and said, "Your daddy asked Jesus to forgive the bad things he had done and to save him, and God took all the bad things away. So your daddy is not in the hole in the ground, he is in heaven with Jesus."

I wish you could have seen the bright smile that lit up her sweet face as she looked up at me and said through her tears, "I thought he was in the hole in the ground."

Understanding their beliefs concerning the spirits helped in teaching them about our own body, soul and spirit as well as about the Holy Spirit. They seemed to feel that it was alright for them to continue to believe in the "benevolent" spirits, since they used them as "white magic" to catch fish, wild pigs etc. However, they failed to think about the fact that those spirits were the ones who would kill their babies if they broke one of their taboos. We could point out that fact to them to help them understand.

I fear that it took a long time before they really accepted the fact that the Creator is God, not Dasawu and Borbit. Understanding their beliefs was invaluable in teaching them about God, heaven, and sin.

In the following few chapters you will get some insight into everyday life with the Citak people.

Chapter 12

FINE DINING WITH THE MIMIKA AND CITAK PEOPLE

"Whatsoever is set before you, eat, asking
no questions."–I Corinthians 10:27

I am often asked if the people to whom we ministered
were offended if we did not eat their food. Although
they were not necessarily offended, it was nevertheless
a good idea to partake of their cuisine if we wanted to be
genuinely received by them.

When I moved from Amar to Senggo in 1975 it was
certainly my desire to be accepted by the Citak people.
I would go to the village every afternoon and sit among
them, visiting and practicing their language. When they
ate, though, they never offered any food to me, which I
found to be unusual.

They had this interesting habit of talking about me as
if I were not there. They probably figured that I did not
understand, which was indeed true for most of the conversation during those early days.

I told them that I wanted to live there with them and
to be one of them. I had already been on the field for 11
years and knew how to eat most of their food. One day
someone mentioned giving me some food. Someone else

responded, "No, she cannot eat our food." So, I picked up some sago, which is one of their staple foods, and placed it on the hot coals. They all watched in fascination as I continued to cook the sago. When it was finished cooking I took it off the fire and began to eat it.

In amazement one of the ladies exclaimed, "She *is* one of us."

I learned a valuable lesson. While not eating their food might not have caused me to be rejected by them, partaking of their diet certainly helped me to become one of them, thus lending greater effectiveness to my witness among them.

Living in a primitive culture gave us the opportunity to eat strange (to us in America) foods such as ants, kangaroo rats, dogs and grub worms, as well as other "tasty" animals. I usually handled this fairly well. I learned that if I just kept talking in order to keep my mind off what I was eating then I could get it to go down before I thought too much about it.

I can remember only one item of food that ever caused me to gag – a clam, of all things. One evening right at dark my colleague, Marge, and I were visiting in the village. The Mimika people had just come in from clamming in the mud. Their practice was to dig the clams out of the mud, and put them on the coals to cook in the shells without bothering to clean them.

I made the big mistake of commenting on the large clams. They generously picked out the largest one and gave it to me. Do you know what mud tastes like? I do. I bit into the clam and was immediately faced with the awful realization that it was full of swamp mud. I began to gag, and my eyes started to water. I wondered what in the world I was going to do.

I got up and began to walk around while talking and keeping my back to the people, all the while trying to figure out what to do next. I knew that if I bit down again I would just get more mud. It was too large to swallow whole but I dared not spit it out. I kept walking and talking and gagging, my eyes still watering. I worked on it, and worked on it, until I finally got it down my throat.

When we got home Marge wanted to know what in the world had been wrong with me, and why I was acting so weird. When I told her what happened she responded, "You should have known better than to brag on their large clams. Of course they were going to give you their best!" I sure wish that she had told me that *before* dinner.

TASTY LIZARDS

The Mimika people loved parties and always put a lot of effort into preparing for them. The men would go out into the jungle and catch large iguanas, which lived in the treetops. The idea was to capture them alive, not kill them, in order to save them until the day of the party.

One brave soul would be elected to climb the tree, grab the critters by the tail and sling them to the ground. Then the men on the ground would chase them, grab them as best they could and hold their mouths shut while another man would tie a vine to their legs. When they had found all that they could, they draped the vine over a pole with the lizards hanging down, wiggling frantically to get free, and bring them back to the village. Usually they would end up with 50-75 of these lively animals, which they would then tie to the pilings of their houses, waiting for the day of the party.

Lizards

The lizards spent their final days and hours tugging at the vines, trying to escape their sentence of death. During that time I avoided going through the village. I was afraid that some of the critters would succeed in freeing themselves, and decide to take their frustrations out on me. I must admit, however, they were quite tasty.

One day the school children put on a "feast" of their own. Of course, their idea of a feast was vastly different from ours. The thing that distinguished this particular feast from others was that the children did most of it themselves. The day arrived and Helen, my coworker, and I were invited to attend the feast. It was held in the school building, which was built about three feet off the ground with a floor that had large cracks in it.

As we sat on the floor the children proudly served us a meal of rice, greens and fish. We did not have electricity, of course, but we did have a pressure lantern that gave very little light. Therefore we could not get a good look at the food, which sometimes could be a real blessing.

A smell hit my nostrils that just wasn't right. I remarked to Helen, "I think the children have been going under the school to use the bathroom."

Helen calmly answered, "It's your food!" She was right! Helen had a unique way of getting rid of her unwanted food by so very graciously "sharing" it with the children. I ate mine!

WORMS, ANYONE?

There was an interesting worm that resided in a certain rotten tree. They said that the best way to eat this worm, called a *tambelok*, was to cut it out of the tree in the heat of the day while it was very warm from the sun, and to devour it right on the spot. They ate it raw, of course. I never had one that way. I had mine in the village where it could at least be washed.

The worm was usually about a foot long, rather transparent and slightly flat looking, with a small sharp snout on the head. The proper way to eat it was to pinch off the snout, use it to cut open the worm, rinse it out a bit in a bowl of water, and then slurp it up like a piece of spaghetti. A word of advice – make sure that you get the first worm, or else bring your own bowl of water.

"Tambelok" worm

Another type of worm that became a part of our diet was the infamous grub worm. Actually, I never had any serious problem with eating them as long as they were cooked crispy. However, boiled grub worms were hard to stomach.

Once we were in an outlying village in a native house with a man and his family, who had been placed there by us as a church planter/teacher. The house, the floor of which had large cracks, stood three to four off the ground. The only light was from a corned beef can, filled with kerosene, which had a twisted rag for a wick. Naturally, it gave very little light.

As we sat on the floor our host served us plates of rice with boiled grub worms. I thought to myself, "How can I eat this?" I really did not want to eat boiled grub worms, but I certainly did not want to offend our host. Then I came up with a brilliant idea. It was dark, right? We were sitting on the floor, right? There were large cracks in the floor, right? I decided that I would just feel around in the rice, pick out the grubs, and stuff them through the cracks. Problem solved! I was very pleased with myself. The grubs disappeared and I ate the rice. Then disaster came. Some pigs discovered the delicious discarded worms, and began eating them as only pigs can do. "Behold," says the Bible, "your sins will find you out."

Sago grubs

The one food experience that stands out the most in my memory was a jungle fruit called *omo*. It grows in the Citak area and tastes a bit like a green apple. The Vakabuis people loved to bring this fruit to me as they knew that I would bring out the salt, which they loved.

Another coworker, Gail Vinje, and I were visiting in the village of Vakabuis when our good friend, a former cannibal named Bidaw, wanted to give us one of the fruits. Having only one, he looked at it, then at us, and his internal calculator told him that something didn't quite add up. He solved the problem by first peeling the fruit, after which he put it in his mouth, bit it in half, gave the outside half to Gail and took the other half out of his mouth and handed it to me. Yes, I ate it with prayer and thanksgiving, with more prayer than thanksgiving, with no ill effects.

KANGAROO RAT

One day Ruth and I were visiting in the village of Vakabuis. I have decided that I can never forgive her for what she did to me there. Normally, when we were in the villages we would eat pretty much what the people ate, which was lots of sago and fish cooked over the open fire. Before leaving home I had decided that on Sunday we would have a real meal. I took rice and a can of corned beef for the occasion.

We had been there several days, and I was really looking forward to our Sunday dinner. However, just before lunch a man came bearing a gift of a roasted kangaroo rat. No problem, I figured. We will just quietly get rid of it and eat our corned beef. Not Ruth! She insisted that we eat the rat. I argued that we had planned for days to have corned beef on Sunday. She argued that the corned beef would keep, but that the rat would spoil.

That was exactly what I wanted it to do. Ruth won the argument, and we ate the rat. No forgiveness for Ruth. Truth be told, I really did not mind the rat. It didn't taste bad at all. It's just that I had been so looking forward to that delicious corned beef. So, I guess I will forgive my good friend, Ruth!

TASTY (NOT) SAGO

The staple food of the Mimika and Citak people is sago, which is the processed center of the sago palm. It is just a starch that tastes like chalk if it is not cooked well. If it *is* cooked well, however, it tastes like cooked chalk.

When I arrived on the field and experienced sago for the first time I thought that I would never be able to eat it joyfully. I put salt in it and the people laughed. I put peanut butter, bananas, jelly or anything else I could think of to give it some flavor. I finally did get used to it and now, as I write this, I am actually hungry for some.

Sago has very little food value, but the people are hungry if they have not had sago. One morning my house help, Timo, came to work looking really down in the mouth. He informed me that he was hungry, and that he had not eaten for three days. I thought, "I can't have someone working for me who has not eaten for three days." I immediately prepared a big breakfast and gave it to him. He gobbled it down, but continued to drag around the house, doing very little.

In a few minutes he said, "Nona, I am hungry. I haven't eaten for three days."

I thought, "What was all that food you just ate?" Then I learned that when they said that they had not eaten, it meant that they had not eaten sago. They could have eaten lots of other things, but unless they had eaten sago, they felt that they had not eaten at all.

Once, I had several of the young men in my home and fed them rice and pork. When the Citak people have something good to eat and lots of it they will eat all that they can hold and then go outside and throw up. They will then come back in and eat again. That night the young men had eaten a very healthy portion of rice and pork. Then I overheard one of them whisper to the others "Let's go. I am hungry."

One day several of us from Senggo were visiting in one of the outlying villages when a man came in with an extremely large fish. The young men with me were standing with their eyes wide open and their mouths watering. Of course, I bought the fish.

At the time we were staying in a native hut with bark, slab-like floors. My room had a flimsy partition, but the bark slabs went from the room where they were into my room. That meant that every time the young men walked around they lifted me up off the floor where I was supposedly sleeping.

They cooked the fish, and we ate it and some sago. I retired to my "room," but they stayed up all night. They certainly could not let that good fish spoil, so they ate it ALL. They would eat, go outside, lifting me off the floor when they stepped on the bark floors, throw up, come back in, lifting me again, eat again, and continue repeating the process all night. The fish was all gone by daylight, and I had not even dozed, but a good time was had by one and all.

GROCERY STORE IN THE JUNGLE

Do you ladies dread grocery shopping day? Let's go with some Citak women to "get groceries." We must leave at the first light of dawn, which is about 5:30 a.m. We walk for about an hour through the swamp in tall grass just to get to our "vehicle," which is a very narrow dugout canoe. It is good to have an experienced Citakker in front because she can use her paddle to shake the grass in order to scare away any snakes that may be lurking about.

I hope you haven't worn your good shoes, for by the time we get to our canoe our legs are caked in mud up to our knees. Also, by all means, do not wear flip flops. They tend to like mud, and will glue themselves into it, leaving you to dig down into the mud with your hands to dig them out. One of the Citak ladies will wash off the mud, after which we climb into the canoe.

If you are used to Mimika canoes, like I was you, will discover that there is a significant difference between them and the Citak canoes. Whereas the Mimika sit to paddle, the Citak people stand, therefore requiring only enough room for their feet. That is a problem for those of us who could never stand up in the canoe, but who at the same time find it difficult to sit down. We finally force our bodies into the canoe, and we are safe. If the canoe turns over they can just turn it upright again, and we will still be there – for we will be stuck!

After about a miserable hour we "park" on the side of the river, pull ourselves out of the canoe and wake up all our limbs before heading into the jungle. This time we want a Citak lady in front with an axe or machete to open the jungle for us. I sure hope you remembered to bring your insect repellent because if you didn't, that which the mosquitoes don't take away the horse flies will. By the way, since we don't have horses here, we call them pig flies instead.

As we stumble along trying to keep our balance and hang on to our camera, we may see a Citak lady in front with a net bag on her head full of things needed for the day while also carrying a child on her shoulders, and all the while she is clearing the jungle with her machete as she goes!

After nearly an hour of this we arrive where the "groceries" are – large sago palms. By this time we are tired, hungry and thirsty. I hope you brought along some food and plenty of water. If not, don't despair, there are various jungle fruits or hearts of palm that we can eat.

Now, let us sit on a log and (gladly) watch. The women proceed to pick out a large tree and cut it down. Some of them begin peeling off the bark while another digs a well with a stick. Still another makes a trough-like thing from the end of a palm branch. A "bucket" is then woven from some more branches. A "sago hoe" is made from a crooked stick with a piece of bamboo fitted on the end and sharp "teeth" cut in it.

The inside of the sago palm is soft, fiber-like material. This is shaved off bit by bit with the sago hoe. Often the women carry their babies on their backs in net bags, which bounce the babies to sleep as they work. Naked toddlers play around, and sometimes sit right down on the sago being processed, which takes several hours.

While the processing is going on, other women are building troughs, of which there are at least two, one on poles about two feet off the ground, and the other fitted to the bottom of the first one and level with the ground. They then find a "sieve," which is conveniently located at the bottom of the trunk of the palm. They pin the sieve to the top trough and place it in the upper trough above the sieve. They then pour dirty swamp water from the well on it and squeeze it, letting the good stuff drain through the sieve, after which they throw away the pulp. A white, clay-like substance settles in the lower trough. They gather it up, and put it into a woven basket or package made from leaves just for this purpose. Sound easy?

Processing sago

It is now about 3:30 in the afternoon. Someone makes a fire from a smoldering piece of wood brought from the village. We put a big hunk of the fresh sago on the fire for dinner before returning home.

Going home with supper

Had we not accompanied the Citak women on their grocery-gathering expedition, they would have made a bivouac and spent the night. They would have also taken time to visit the "meat department," which entails cutting into a large, rotten sago palm and gathering the large grubs that live inside it, or else looking for large ants in the trees, or else fishing along the river. However, we are happy to pass up the meat on this trip, because by now, all we want is to take a bath and go to bed.

We arrive home about 5:00 p.m., sun-blistered, tired, thirsty, hungry and needing medicine for all our bites and scratches, and feeling *very* thankful that we have been privileged to have been born in America. We have gathered enough sago to last an average family about three days. Thus, pretty soon, it will be time to go again to the grocery store in the jungle.

By the way, wouldn't you love to be on hand to observe when these dear Citak ladies get their first glimpse of heaven?

Chapter 13

LIVING (OR DYING) WITH HOUSE HELP

MODERN CONVENIENCES IN THE JUNGLE

"What is a poor missionary doing with house help?" some folks might ask. "I sure wish I were a missionary, so I could have someone to do my housework." That is why we seldom mentioned house help to our friends and supporters in America. Believe me, most days we would gladly trade our house help for an automatic washer and dryer, electric refrigerator, running hot water, and we wouldn't even need a dishwasher!

But then, I did have running hot water. Timo, my house help, would come early each morning and light a fire under a 55-gallon drum that had the top cut out, and a copper tube fitted into it. Requiring a sizable supply of firewood for that, he had to go out in the jungle to cut it. After the water got hot he would fill a bucket, and "run" it into the house for washing dishes, or into the wringer washing machine for washing clothes. In the early years we washed clothes by hand. Later, my "automatic" washing machine was Timo washing in the wringer machine, and the "dryer" was furnished by the Lord.

I even had a "self-defrosting" refrigerator. However, it defrosted on its own timetable, not on mine. It ran, when it wanted to, on kerosene. Timo pumped kerosene from the drum once a week and filled the tank at the bottom of the refrigerator. The wick had to be cleaned often, and changed periodically, which I had to do myself. If there was water or dirt in the kerosene, which there quite often was, the wick would clog, and the entire house would fill with black, stinky smoke and the refrigerator defrosted. That involved about half a day to take it all apart and clean it, and try to get it to work again, which I had to do myself. Then there was the smoky house to deal with. I did NOT like that refrigerator.

DON'T WATCH THE HOUSE HELP

It appears to be an unspoken rule among house help to never do anything that they were not specifically told to do. When asked why they didn't do something, the standard answer they gave was, "You didn't tell me to."

Once there was a wad of paper on the floor for several days right in the same spot. I decided to watch the house girl when she swept. She very carefully picked up the paper, swept the floor, and then put the paper right back where she had found it. I asked her why she didn't put it in the trash and she said, you guessed it, "You didn't tell me to."

As a rule, however, one should never stay around to watch the house help work. Once I came in when a small boy was washing dishes. I caught him washing the mud off his feet with the dishcloth. They don't understand the difference in dishcloths, floor rags, towels, etc. To them, a rag is a rag.

And never, never watch when your house help handles food, because it could be bad for your health – or theirs. After returning from furlough with a lovely set of very sharp knives, I came into the kitchen one day after Timo had already cut up cabbage for cole slaw. I began to cut up some carrots and almost cut my hand, at which point I mentioned to him how sharp the new knives were. Timo held out his hands and said, "Yeah, I know. I cut off all my fingernails while cutting up the cabbage." Cole slaw, anyone? Crunchy cole slaw, that is. By the way, cole slaw was removed from the menu that day.

A man named Torka worked for me and married a woman named Tabita, who went to work for my coworker Gail, whose house was just across the yard from mine. One day when Gail was at the hospital, Tabita came running across the yard holding her eyes and screaming, "I can't see! I can't see!" Torka panicked and so did I. We had no idea what was wrong, and she was in such a panic that she couldn't tell us for a while. She just kept screaming, "My eyes, my eyes!"

When we finally got her calmed down enough to talk coherently I asked, "What were you doing?"

She replied, "I was peeling onions." As you have probably already surmised, that was her first time performing that particular chore.

DON'T USE MY TOOTHBRUSH

One thing one always teaches people who work inside the house is – "Don't use my toothbrush, comb, brush, or razor." You can always tell when they use the comb, brush or razor because of the dirt and hair, but how does one know when your toothbrush has been used?

At Amar our bathroom was off the side of the house with a boardwalk going out to it. So, it opened to the outside. One day some little boys had a fight and their favorite pass time was telling on each other. One boy came and told me that one of the other boys had been sneaking in every day and using my toothbrush! It was the first time in his life to brush his teeth. It was a long time before I could brush my teeth without gagging.

ADOPTED CHILDREN

One of the first things to learn is not to allow them to make you think that they are your 'adopted' children. Actually, their word for what we call "house help" was "adopted child." Don't be fooled into thinking that is cute. If you do, you will find yourself being expected to fully support them along with their family. To avoid that, you must make it clear to them that they work, you pay them a salary, and then they support their family with that salary that they have earned. However, you do usually end up sending their children to school.

The people who worked in our houses knew absolutely everything about us and believe me, through them, everyone in the village also knew. It was a wonderful opportunity to have a witness by the way we lived before them. Having them around for much of the day also meant that we grew to love them, well, like "adopted" children.

Chapter 14

TRAVELING IN PAPUA

DUGOUT CANOES

When you are young and foolish you do foolish things. When at Amar our mode of travel was either by foot along the beach or by dugout canoe. Amar was located right on the lovely beach. To go by canoe from Amar to the government post at Kokonao took about 24 hours. By airplane it took about 15 minutes.

For a couple of months a year the ocean was relatively calm. During that season we could travel on the ocean. Looking back on it now, we were very foolish. We would hire paddlers to take us out through the breakers into the calm sea – without life jackets. I did not know how to swim. God takes care of foolish people!

No one knew that we were out there. Later the mission ruled that we must not go out on the ocean without informing someone on the radio where we were going and when we expected to arrive. Also, we were required to wear life jackets. That was after several years of being foolish!

Sometimes Marge and I would walk along the beach while the paddlers would paddle the canoe carrying our belongings. When we would come to the mouth of a river they would come in, take us across, and then go back out again.

Sleeping on the beach wasn't too much fun either. Sand tends to stick to perspiration making one very uncomfortable.

Amar canoe

This is an excerpt from my journal, dated Feb. 28, 1969:

"We went to Mupuruka today. We walked along the beach, and nearly starved for a drink before we got back. We took the picnic jug, but the men with us didn't take any water so we had to share, and had about one tenth as much as we needed. The people in the village gave Marge and me coconut water in a dirty glass and we guzzled it down without a thought about the possibility of ameba, and thoroughly enjoyed it. They also gave us hot horrible half ripe watermelon, which we also thoroughly enjoyed.

We arrived home late that afternoon, red, blistered, tired and very thirsty. We just about drank the drums dry.

Now after a good drink, a nice refreshing shower, and a bed, I feel great. Getting home and relaxing after a trip like that seems give a small hint of what heaven will be like when we get there.

On the way home we met an old couple. His canoe was old and horrible looking. His wife and he were coming to Amar. He wanted to go on the ocean. She wanted to go by river because she was afraid of the waves and the old canoe. Well, he just threw her overboard. She got back in and threw him overboard. He got mad and cut the canoe to pieces with his machete. They made it to shore, where she beat him with a stick, and that was when we arrived. He said it was a good thing they were close to shore when he cut up the canoe or she would be dead. She called him an animal and a lot of other ugly things. She returned to Mupuruka, and he came with us, and we left the sinking canoe. Always some excitement."

The Mimika people did not put forth any more effort that absolutely necessary when doing anything. During the season when the ocean was too rough to travel we had to go by river. Being close to the ocean, the rivers were affected by the tides, which the people took full advantage of. We never left Amar until the tide started coming in. Then no matter what time of day or night it was, we started out up river, going along with the tide which did not require much energy to paddle. Then when we arrived at the point where we would start back down river, we would sit there for however long it took, and regardless of the time of night, waiting for the tide to start out again. So, we might find ourselves just sitting in the very uncomfortable canoe in the middle of the night waiting for the tide to take us home.

BOATS WITH OUTBOARD MOTORS

At Senggo we had the luxury of boats with outboard motors, and even had men to operate them for us. That made traveling to the outlying village much more enjoyable. Senggo was far from the ocean so we did not go on the ocean. However, we did continue to wear life jackets.

Many hours and days were spent in the boats and I loved traveling through the jungle up the quiet rivers. We would see pretty birds and sometimes crocodiles. We would tie up the boat under a tree for our picnic on the way.

Visiting the "facilities" was always interesting and sometimes challenging. Sometimes the water level was high, making it near to impossible to get out of the boat and go into the jungle. Other times the water level was low, making it even more challenging, as there was a muddy bank to negotiate.

I remember once when Siprianus and Titus went through mud above their knees into the jungle, found a log, placed it from the boat to the bank, and then stood in the mud while holding my hand as I crossed free of the mud to the bank. What wonderful gentlemen!

FLOAT PLANE

Since we did not have roads, we depended on the airplane to bring our supplies and mail, or take us out when we needed to go. Sometimes if a village were located on a large river, we could have the float plane pilot take us. We did not do that too often as the cost of getting the float plane to Senggo was expensive.

This is an excerpt from Ruth Dougherty's letter after returning from a trip to Vakabuis:

"I've got a couple of savages on board!" announced our pilot to the whole island over his shortwave radio after Margaret and I boarded the MAF float plane. No doubt he was justified in this slam since we had just offered him a chocolate covered wood grub and dirty river water for his snack. However, it may have been our lovely appearance and fragrance after two weeks in the primitive Brazza village of Vakabuis that prompted such a comment."

Float plane

AIRPLANE ON WHEELS

We had a dirt airstrip at Senggo, so the small Cessna plane could land there. We could not have stayed at Senggo without the pilots and the airplanes, and we cannot express our appreciation for them too much. It was always exciting to see the airplane coming our way, especially when we expected mail from home. There was only one thing worse that having the pilot forget the mail. It was if he did not forget it – there was not any mail to bring.

We always had a cold drink and a snack for the pilot, and Gail had threatened that if he forgot the mail, the "chocolate chips" in his cookies would be ex-lax! The pilots did not forget our mail!

Wheel plane

Chapter 15

DISCOURAGED? ME? NO WAY!

I was so very excited about the prospects of being a missionary. Discouragement was not in my vocabulary. If I ever achieved that greatly anticipated goal of being a missionary there was no way I would ever be discouraged. How could a missionary be discouraged? Was I ever the most naïve future missionary!

I was working hard at raising my initial 1963 and was participating in a big Missions Conference at Mikado Baptist Church in Macon, Ga. By the way, that church was the first to take my support and continued to support me for the next 41 years. What a record! There were several support in other churches also that supported me for the entire 40 years on the field. Someone at that conference was speaking about how to pray for missionaries, and one of her points was to pray that the missionaries would not be discouraged.

I was thinking, "What? A discouraged missionary? No way." My time to speak followed that speaker. I stood before that large church with all the excitement of a future missionary and said, "You don't need to pray for ME about that." I could not imagine being discouraged if God gave me the privilege of being a missionary! After I sat down a very wise veteran missionary came to me and gave me some of the best advice I ever received. She said, "You had better shut up."

Back then prospective missionaries just answered God's call and went, having very little idea about what we were getting into. People didn't make survey trips or visit the fields before going on a permanent basis. We just went in response to God's leading and figured things out along the way. I was probably more naïve than most, and went out with lots of grandiose ideas about what life as a missionary would be. What a surprise it was to me to arrive on the field and to learn very quickly that *some* of the missionaries did not want another single lady there. That was something that had to be dealt with for the next 40 plus years on the field.

So, as quite a surprise to me, my first bout with discouragement came almost immediately. I learned quickly that missionaries do indeed become discouraged. I really should have already known that because that was not my first experience with discouragement.

ANONYMOUS LETTER

It was during my first year of college. I was eighteen years old adjusting to living away from home, learning to work and pay my own way including paying the college tuition. I had a great job as Medical Secretary in the local hospital. One day a letter appeared out of nowhere on the desk at the nurses' station where I worked. It was addressed to me, and it was not signed. The writer basically told me that I should not be working at the hospital among such "sinners." They also said that I should take off my ungodly heathen earrings, and let my hair grow out! It said something about really being serious about being a missionary, implying that I was not. I was a bundle of hurt, anger, frustration and depression.

I did not present a very pleasant sight, and declared that I was not going to school another day! An unsaved doctor appeared at the station just in time to witness the angry tirade I was presenting. Isn't it amazing how sometimes God uses unsaved people to teach us our best lessons. He asked what was wrong, and I slammed the letter down in front of him and said, "Read that!" He read it and ordered me to sit down and very sternly asked, "Why are you going to college?" "So I can be a missionary." "Who are you going to be a missionary for?" "God, of course." "Then why do you want to quit because of some person who refused to sign their name tries to discourage you?" Of course, when he put it that way, I decided that whoever wrote that letter would not discourage me.

Do missionaries get discouraged? You bet they do. I doubt if there has ever been a missionary who had not been discouraged at some time or other. Come to think about it, I doubt if there is anyone, missionary or not, who has not been discouraged. A word to missionaries reading this. Not IF, but WHEN, you become discouraged, just remember that you would have tough times no matter where you are. Remember that tough times in God's will are sure a lot better than tough times out of His will. So hang in there!

ALONE AT AMAR

I had been alone on the station at Amar in the Mimika tribe for about two years. My co-worker, Marge Smith had not been able to return following her furlough due to sickness in her family. I could write the book on loneliness.

The ministry at Amar was difficult, the people for the most part unresponsive. At the end of the two years alone, the mission informed me that I would not be allowed to return there. I cried every day during the week of our annual conference, and felt like a failure being told by the mission leaders that I could not remain at Amar alone.

The mission had just reopened the ministry in the Citak tribe at Senggo and our doctor, Ken Dresser and his wife Sylvia, along with Clarence and Twila Gillett and others who had cleared the land for the airstrip, built the small hospital and missionary houses.

The Citak people were open and responsive. I was invited to move to Senggo and my ministry would be to analyze the language, reduce it to writing, and translate Scripture. I arrived emotionally down, but pretty soon began to get excited about the ministry there.

"HE CARES FOR YOU"

Since there was no house for me I was put into a "building." It had four rooms all in a row, with windows all the way around. There was no glass in the windows, but at least it did have screens. I had a bedroom, a living room, a kitchen and a study. The study being on the end had windows or screens on three sides.

I settled in and began working on analyzing and learning the Citak language. That was before computers, so everything was done by hand. The work was progressing well, and I was feeling great. All of my handwritten work was spread out on the table in the study. Then disaster hit!

I was awakened in the middle of the night by a big rain storm, with the wind whipping around all directions. I got up and started through the "house" with my flashlight to check on things. Remember, there was no glass in the windows. I was able to move things around in the living room to get them out of the rain. The wind had blown the door open to the kitchen which was no big problem since the floor had large cracks in it and the rain just washed the floors.

Then I went into the study. To my dismay, I found my work completely soaked. I estimated that at least 90% of my hard work was destroyed. At that instance, I just lost it! I was discouraged and frustrated and *very* angry at God. I told Him, "I did all that for You and You don't even care. You promised never to leave me and You did. You said that You would go with me to the end and You didn't. You put me in the middle of this jungle and You don't even remember where You put me."

While I was pouring out my feelings to God, I was putting all my work on the floor under the table as the only dry place in the room. Then I returned to bed. I was crying in my pillow, feeling so forsaken by God, when a large puff of wind came whipping through, and something hit me on the head! I thought, "That's the last straw!" I turned on my flashlight to see what it was. It was a small plaque that I had hanging over my bed that read, "He Cares For You."

I began laughing through my tears and said, "O.K., Lord. I get it. Thank you." So I learned that for some people, God speaks to in a still small voice. Others of us, however, He konks on the head.

I am not proud of how angry I was at God and for the things I said to Him. By the way, I was accusing Him of not being there, yet I was talking to Him. I am proud of what I learned about Him that night. He is a big God and can take it when we need to pour out the thoughts of our heart to Him. He will find a way to get through to us. And He has a sense of humor. What a God we have!

Let me encourage you not to be afraid to tell Him just how you feel remembering that He already knows the thoughts of your heart, so you may as well go ahead and voice them. You will find a listening ear from One

Who loves you perfectly. Nothing you say to Him can change that.

This was written in my diary during on another especially difficult time:

"I can't see what I am writing for the tears – foolish tears. Down deep in my heart I know that God is near and I am holding tightly to that thin thread of faith – but why does He seem so far away. I <u>feel</u> like He put me here, set me down and forgot all about me and left me for Satan to try, grind and break."

I had copied this from an unknown source:

"No matter the way be sometimes dark, no matter thought the cost be sometimes great, He knoweth how I best shall reach the mark – the way that leads to Him must needs be straight."

DEPRESSION TOO DEEP TO TELL

Another time that is too personal to tell anyone about, I experienced a period of severe depression because of a situation that had happened on the field. I got up excited that the airplane was scheduled to come that day, and we always looked forward to that, mainly because it meant getting mail! My thrill of getting mail was shattered by one letter. That letter sent me into the deepest valley of discouragement and despair I have ever known. I felt worse than Jonah drowning in the belly of the whale. Elijah under the juniper tree was living in victory in comparison to how I felt. I wanted to die.

I fell literally on the floor on my face and cried and wept until I could cry no more, and I was totally exhausted. I did not want to live. I did not want to be a missionary any more. I wanted to quit. God was nowhere to be found and I felt more alone than ever in my life.

There was no pastor I could call on. There was nowhere to go to get away. I was in the jungle with no way out and nowhere to go, and God didn't just seem far away, it felt as if He did not exist.

I could not pray. I couldn't even think. The writer of the letter was far away. It was an entire year before that could even be discussed or attempted to resolve.

On my desk – 1986

"Be still my soul; though future ways are shrouded;
What matters it since thou dost walk with Him;
Would life be sweeter were its skies unclouded;
Or safer were its future no more dim?
Nor so, my soul, to have all limits ended;
To see or know all would not give thee rest;
'Twill better be on to Him have depended;
And can He, could He, leave His child unblest?"

I included this chapter to be an encouragement to young missionaries – or anyone for that matter. Discouragements WILL come. For some of them, we may never know what God's purpose was. As for others, He will reveal the meaning to us. The thing that kept me on the field during that time was the fact that I KNEW that if I quit I would be out of God's will and that scared me.

In times of discouragement we learn to cling more closely to Him and will eventually find Him and ever present help. He gave me Jeremiah 29:11 *"For I know the thoughts that I think toward you, saith the Lord, thoughts of peace, and not of evil, to give you an expected end."*

Discouraged missionary – He IS with you and He does love you, and He has plans for your future.

SHOW ME THY HANDS

LORD, when I am weary with toiling
And burdensome seem Thy commands,
If my load should lead to complaining,
LORD, show me Thy hands
Thy nail-pierced hands
Thy cross-torn hands;
My SAVIOUR, show me Thy hands.
CHRIST, if ever my footsteps should falter
And I be prepared for retreat,
If desert and thorn cause lamenting,
LORD, show me Thy feet,
Thy bleeding feet,
Thy nail-scarred feet;
My JESUS, show me Thy feet.
LORD, when I am sorely wounded
With battle and toil of the day,
And I complain of my suffering,
LORD, let me hear Thee say,
"Behold My side,
My spear-pierced side,
My side that was wounded for Thee."
My GOD, dare I show Thee
My hands and my feet?

-Selected. Author unknown

Chapter 16

SERMONS WORTH REMEMBERING— OR FORGETTING

"I feel more like I do now, than when I first came in." Unknown.

The people had very little knowledge of Scripture, and even less knowledge about how to preach. Being a lady, it was for certain that I could not preach, so our churches were completely indigenous from the beginning. That was a good thing, but did result in sermons that were quite entertaining, and sometimes actual heresy when they had not understood the lesson.

I learned very early after teaching a lesson not to ask, "Did you understand?" They always answered, "Yes." However when they preached, it was obvious that they had not understood. So I learned to ask specific questions about the lesson, but often it became clear that they still had not really understood.

IN THE BEGINNING WAS THE WELL.....

During my time at Amar, a young man named Paskalis was in my Bible class. One day the students were encouraged to give their testimony. This was the first time that Pas had ever given a testimony, but he seemed very confident about what to do. He began by reading John 1:1. *"In the beginning was the Word, and the Word was with God, and the Word was God."*

Pas was from the Mimika tribe and had a limited knowledge of Indonesian. He was He thought *"kalam"* (*word*) was *"kolam"* (well). speaking in Indonesian, and had one major problem. He spoke at length about a "well" being from the beginning, being with God, and being God. He spoke with confidence and it made for an interesting but completely meaningless testimony. He seemed to feel that he had done a great job.

ONE BODY TO BE BAPTIZED

Another man from Amar named Esau preached on Ephesians 4:4-5. *"There is one body, and one Spirit even as ye are called in one hope of your calling. One Lord, one faith, and one baptism,"* We were preparing for a baptismal service, so Esau felt that it would be a good thing to preach on baptism. He said, "Friends, here is clear proof. You have only one body. The word of God says so. There is one body, one faith, and one baptism. Friends, there is one baptism and you who want to be baptized, remember, you have only one body to do it with!"

ADULTERY?

Another young man was scheduled to preach one Sunday and had spent the week preparing. He planned to preach about the lady taken in adultery in John chapter 8. Sunday arrived and we were about to begin the service. He went to Marge and asked, "What does adultery mean?"

HEAVEN

The people at Senggo lived in huts made from palm stem walls, bark floors and thatched roofs. They had no furniture, and slept on mats the women had woven from leaves. They cooked inside the house on an open fire built on dirt which they had brought in from the outside. Each family unit had their own fire. As several families usually lived together in one room and each had their own fire, all that smoke had to go somewhere. It found its way up and out through the thatched roof.

They had been in our houses, and had sat on our chairs and seen our furniture. In the beginning they were pretty fascinated by all the "stuff" in our homes. One day Abdon was preaching about Heaven and said, "In Heaven everybody will have beds and chairs!" I was thinking, "Do you ever have a surprise coming."

Several years later he was preaching again on Heaven and said, "When we get to Heaven we will all have radios and airplanes." Great to see spiritual growth!

THE BIBLE IN THE GARDEN OF EDEN?

One thing we had to learn was that if we did not explain something really well and they did not understand it, then they would just make it up. It would have been great if they had just asked questions, but that was a foreign concept to them. I think that they thought that asking a question would have been rude, as it would have indicated that I had not explained it well. I wish they had asked questions!

For example, the preachers would almost always preface their sermons with "The Nona said..." I am Nona. I thought, "This won't do." So I called them in and showed them my Bible and also the Indonesian Bible, and explained to them that this was God's Word. I told them that all that I had been teaching them came from this book. I explained to them that we would translate it into their language too so they could read it for themselves. In the meantime, I was teaching them what it said. "So," I said, "Don't say this is from Nona, but tell the people that it is God's Word." That sounded clear enough to me.

The next Sunday Noak began to preach and said, "Do you think that the things we have been telling you came from Nona? No, it did not come from her. She has a book, and in it is God's words. She will translate it into our language so we can read it. So, what she has been teaching us is from the Book from God. God left it in the Garden of Eden with Adam and Eve!" Obviously some more explanations were in order.

LEANING AGAINST THE WALL

In the beginning the preachers were self-conscious and shy about preaching. I remember one in particular. He would go over to the side of the church, lean against the wall and preach to the other side of the church. It was almost impossible to get him to stand in front of the church and preach facing the congregation.

Teaching them to use pictures was also a challenge. They would hold the picture right in front of their face, with it facing them. The audience could see only the back of the picture. It was like they could not teach it without looking at the picture themselves.

It was a joy to watch them grow in their knowledge of Scripture, and also in their confidence. However, it was not easy impressing on them the need to study. They loved the story about Zacheus, and we always knew when they had not prepared. It was always obvious when several of them had not studied, for we would hear once again another sermon on Zacheus!

GRAPE-BEARING FIG TREE

One Sunday Joni decided to preach from a passage that had not yet been translated, so he read it in the Indonesian language which he understood very little. He preached in Citak about a tree named "bush" that had thorns on it, and another tree named "fig" that had lots of grapes on it.

He ended his very informative message with this testimony. "I cried last night because I was thinking about my sins. I had been thinking too much about getting clothes for myself and I was afraid that I was about to die. I am sure that I will die at night because I was born at night. People who were born in the daytime will die in the daytime."

His closing illustration really spoke to my heart. "Look over there at those curtains," he said. "They are green. My shirt is white. They are different colors. Look at those missionaries. Their skins are white and ours are black. Therefore, you must train your children." I didn't get it either.

DON'T DRINK BITTER WATER

Esau gave a lesson one morning. It was worse than terrible. He had the Israelites digging wells at Marah, and Moses threw a tree in it and it turned into wine and they drank it all! The lesson was, "Friends, we also don't want to drink bitter water. If we do we will be dizzy."

Other memorable sermon quotations:

"Adam and Eve did not have to work for their food. It was suddenly cooked and setting before them."

"Satan lives out in the jungle and he usually chops people up with his machete."

"If you giggle when someone is praying, God will strike you dead."

"If you go to the jungle on Sunday instead of coming to church a wild boar will attack you, and you can't get on that narrow road that goes to heaven."

It was a joy to watch several of the men, including Piet, Titus and Abdon grow in their preaching ability. They started out preaching five-minute sermons that said almost nothing of value. In time, their preaching became filled with knowledge, and with the power of the Holy Spirit. Many people have been led to a saving faith in the Lord through their Spirit filled preaching.

When the missionaries had all gone from Senggo, there were churches in every one of the villages in the Citak and Tamnim tribes, all being pastored by nationals. Some of these pastors still cannot read, and all of them desperately need training. None of them have a salary, but God is using them to build His church there.

We rejoice to know that they have the Holy Spirit to teach them in order for them to teach their people.

MY TEACHING

Then there were my stories and lessons. It is easy for us to take a lot for granted, and difficult to remember that they have had no background about the lessons being taught. Sometimes I would teach a story, and from the blank looks on their faces would know that it had not made sense to them. Then there were others that they loved to hear over and over again.

One of those stories was the story about the Egyptian plagues. They knew ALL about frogs, boils, lice, etc., and never failed to thoroughly enjoy hearing the story again and again,

Every child loves a good object lesson complete with all the props. The Citak children were no exception, but I learned that one needs to be careful – really careful.

Once, while teaching about Elijah, I prepared a great way to illustrate Elijah calling fire down from heaven. It involved using a highly flammable alcohol. When using a pressure lantern, you must first heat the kerosene before igniting the lantern. That is done by pouring a small amount of highly flammable alcohol into a small container in the lantern, lighting it, and allowing it to burn for a few minutes to heat it before turning on the lantern.

The alcohol is clear and looks like water. Perfect for my illustration. The classroom had dirt floors. Also perfect. While I was telling the story I made a small "altar" on the floor with pebbles, put small sticks on it, dug the "trench," and poured the "water" on the sacrifice. As this was on the floor, the children were all standing totally engrossed in anticipation of the "miracle" that was about to happen.

Then the story developed until the big moment came for fire to come down from heaven. I struck a match and dropped it on the altar. Pandemonium broke loose! The "water" exploded into flames, and ear piercing screams came from the children, and they ALL ran screaming from the room. I went out and gathered them all together again, and reassured them that they were definitely not about to die.

Several years later they came up with their own way to illustrate the story. Theirs made mine look like child's play. They built an "altar" from dry palm branches. It looked like an Indian teepee. They also piled up dry branches inside it. Then they poured kerosene on all of it, which was much safer than the flammable alcohol!

Then they soaked a rope with kerosene and sent a small boy up a coconut tree a short distance way, carrying the end of the rope. The other end was tied to the "altar". This was all done after dark for effect. At the appropriate time the boy lit the rope and sent the fire down from the top of the tree down the rope onto the "altar". Very effective.

The Citak people loved pictures, of course. Naturally, some of the things in the pictures were foreign to them and had to be explained. They loved the picture of Noah and the ark, and attempted to pick out the animals. They seemed to have no concept of size. For example, the fact that a rat was beside an elephant meant little to them, and since they had never seen an elephant, both animals were rats.

DRAMA ANYONE?

I began doing something very different for them. I would tell the story and they have the children act it out. They loved it.

One day the lesson was about Joseph and Potiphar's wife. Every girl absolutely refused to be Potiphar's wife, so I decided that I would have to play that part. "Joseph" came in on cue and I began to "flirt" with him. I motioned for him to come to me–and he came! YIKES! I think that he was afraid not to do as the Nona said! I did explain that he was supposed to run away.

In the chapter on "Christmas at Senggo" I will tell more about my experience at directing a drama.

Chapter 17

FIRST CONVERTS

W hen I arrived at Senggo, I was encouraged to find the people there to be responsive. They seemed very anxious to hear what we had to tell them. I felt that all I had to do was learn the language, love them, give them the gospel, and they would be saved. I began working hard to analyze and learn the language. When I began to have classes the people flocked in to hear what I had to say, even when my proficiency in the language was lacking. I feel that I taught the same thing for two to three years with no results. One day Pemar said, "Nona, you tell us that all the time." I thought, "Then do something about it!" I wondered if they would ever understand and respond.

They loved to hear the Bible stories, and the life of Jesus. When I would tell them the story of the healing of the blind man, they would close their eyes tightly and ask, "He was blind like this?" and then open them and ask, "Then he could see like this?"

When hearing about the resurrection, they would pinch their arms and ask, "This stuff also rose from the dead?"

Other questions were, "He walked right on top of the water?" "He made the storm stop by just telling it to?" They asked me, "Have you ever met Jesus?" "No." "Did He speak your language? "No." "Was He from your tribe?"

"No." The looks on their faces let me know that I was not making any sense at all to them.

Try to imagine that you are one of those people, and a strange looking person comes in and tells you that someone named God, who lives way up in the sky somewhere, created all the things that you see. That God loves you and sent me here to tell you. He has a really nice village up there where no one gets sick or hungry; no one fights, cries, or dies. God wants you to come and live with Him in his nice village. However, He will not allow the least bad thing into His village.

They readily admitted that they had all done bad things so were excluded from entrance into God's village. Then I would tell then the good news about the substitutionary death of Jesus. That was when I lost them.

It felt like a physical barrier came between us and it did not make sense to them that someone whom even I had never seen, didn't speak my language, wasn't from my tribe, and lived a long, long time ago died for them.

We knew that only the Holy Spirit could open their hearts to understand such a thing as that. So we prayed.... and prayed.

A number of people, mostly men who worked with me in the language, had already become Christians. Those men were leading the church services.

It seemed almost overnight that the light shone through. The people began coming in groups saying that they wanted to confess their sins to God, and ask for forgiveness. Seeing a conviction of sin was amazing. So many were coming that we had to divide them up between myself, other missionaries and the church leaders.

It spread across the airstrip at the village of Tamnim, where one of the church leaders there, Matius, and his mother brought about half the village to us to pray with them. Then it spread to the outlying villages.

There is no greater thrill than watching the work of the Holy Spirit as He opens hearts to understand what seems to be impossible. We missionaries cannot take any credit for what God did, but we certainly can rejoice because He allowed us to witness the working of His power among the Citak people.

PIRI – CONFESS SINS

In the beginning the people did not understand the difference between "sins" and "the sin nature." One Sunday morning I was sitting beside Piri during the church service. She fidgeted so much that I thought that she must be sick. When Abdon barely began the invitation her hand shot up.

She said that she really needed to confess her sins to God. I invited her to do so. She went something like this, as she counted them off on her fingers, "This is when I stole someone's catfish. This is when I got angry at my husband. This is when I stole someone's fish. This is when I put a curse on Apaya. This is when I beat my kids. This is when I stole sago." And on and on she went.

She proceeded to confess until she had named all her fingers. Then she held up her feet one at a time and named all her toes. At that point she didn't know where else to go since that is as far as they can count. I was thinking, "This is becoming very interesting."

When she had run out of things to name she hesitated a bit, and then said, "Lord, there are a whole lot more in there!" After she completed her prayer, she breathed a big sigh of relief and said, "Now I can go to Heaven, can't I?" "You sure can," I assured her.

Here is an excerpt from my journal in 1984:

"This past week has been really exciting as we have watched God work among the Senggo people. Church leaders began confessing sin, then villagers began calling the church leaders for prayer – some about sin in their lives, some for salvation, and some because of fear or sickness. We missionaries were called also, but mostly it was the church leaders. Yesterday, Sunday, we had an overflow crowd in church – over 500 – and about 20 people were saved plus several Christians who wanted prayer about sin. Others requested baptism. About 20 were saved after Ruth Dougherty's and my ladies' classes on Friday.

"Today we got word that 21 people made professions of faith in Christ at the village of Komasma yesterday."

Here is another excerpt from my journal from the Vakabuis village in Sept. 1985:

"Alfons preached on the death, burial and resurrection of Christ. He told them why Christ died and what they must do in order to go to heaven. He told them that they must confess their sins and one fellow started confessing right in the middle of the service. He thought he had to confess to the others and didn't understand that he was supposed to confess to God. After discussing it with them and helping them to understand, two men were saved. Our first converts in Vakabuis, and we were very excited."

From my journal in 1987:

"We had our first converts at Wabak. New church building in Abaw and Binam. Senggo Citak church called its first pastor with a starting salary Rp. 10,000/mo." (About $1.)

From our Senggo Annual Report to the Field Conference in 1985:

"120 confessions. 245 baptisms."

From the Report in 1986:

"87 professions. 78 baptisms 3014 attending services in Citak area."

Those years were exciting times as we witnessed the moving of the Holy Spirit as He opened their hearts to understand, to see genuine conviction of sin, and to see them come to the Lord for salvation.

As I have already stated, none of us can take any credit for what God did in the Citak tribe during those years. All of us are so amazed and honored that God even allowed us the privilege to be His ambassadors there. The glory and praise go to the One Who had loved the Citak people from the beginning.

Chapter 18

FIRST BAPTISMS

It was exciting to arrive at the time for our first baptisms. We taught them as well as we knew how, but it appeared that Satan also was busy "teaching" them. We hesitated to baptize too soon for fear that they would not understand. Then in spite of all the teaching and explaining over and over again, many of them continued to put too great an emphasis on baptism, and when asked if they were saved, often they would answer, "I have been baptized."

The church formed a committee to examine the candidates for baptism, and were they ever rough! My good friend, Pemar, went through the class three times before she was approved. The reason, "Her mouth is too big." I rejoiced that I did not have to be accepted by that group!

As the people began to understand and accept Christ as their Savior, it was always an exciting day when a baptismal service was held. During the rainy season it was no problem to find a nice river in which to baptize. However, during the dry season it became more of a challenge to find enough water without going a long way to the large river.

On one of those occasions the men had found a "hole" that was surrounded by tall grass. I insisted that they go with a stick and shake it all around to scare away any snakes that just might be lurking in the grass waiting for a chance to bite me.

Baptizing in a hole

Also, sometimes, between 50 and 150 people may be baptized at the same time. That became very uncomfortable standing in the hot sun with high humidity while waiting for all of the people to be baptized. So, three or four men would baptize at the same time.

Baptizing three people at a time

I remember once when we had to walk through the muddy swamp to the spot where the baptism was to take place. Then we stood on logs while hanging on to a tree branch while the people were being baptized.

Baptizing in the swamp

TITUS' FIRST BAPTISM

Titus was the first Citakker at Senggo to baptize converts. We had about 50 to be baptized and people were lined up on each side of the river. Titus went down into the water and the first convert was led down. Titus put his hand up in the air, hesitated briefly, then looked at me and asked, "What is it that I am supposed to say?" I whispered, "In the Name of the Father." He repeated it and then looked up at me. I said, "In the Name of the Son." Then, "In the name of the Holy Spirit." I made sure he had it all learned well before the next baptismal service.

Chapter 19

FIRST COMMUNION

W e felt that the time had come to teach them about communion and have the first Communion Service. I taught them as well as I could and thought that they had understood. No scripture had been translated so they depended on what was being taught.

The big day arrived and we missionaries were all excited. A missionary without a camera is not a missionary at all, so we armed ourselves with our cameras to record the big event. Filled with anticipation, we all walked down to the church.

Surprise awaited us. The church was empty. The village was empty. The pastor of the church, Titus, was nowhere to be found. In fact, nobody could be found. Only a chicken here and a chicken there were seen.

It turned out that they had heard the part of the lesson about "eating" or "drinking" unworthily and gotten it in their minds that if they partook of communion they would all die. The entire village had run into the jungle to hide—including Titus.

Back to the drawing board and more teaching.

They did learn the meaning of communion and then began to regular communion services.

Communion service. Pemar in dark dress.

Chapter 20

WEDDINGS, MIMIKA
& CITAK STYLE

SECRET WEDDING

We had our first Mimika wedding at Amar and it was exciting, to say the least. Our Field Chairman and his wife came to Amar to perform the ceremony. The village chief who was from the opposing religion there came on Saturday very upset, saying that we could not marry them because the bride could not leave their church. Actually, she already had!

He was causing such an uproar until we feared he would interrupt the ceremony on Sunday morning, so we decided to have the ceremony on Saturday afternoon – in secret. We quietly got word to the Christians to come to our house.

I took the bride and dressed her in one of my dresses, and we hid the groom in the pantry to dress, and had a very pretty first Christian wedding in our living room.

Since we were afraid for the newlyweds to return to the village that night we brought their sleeping mats and turned our storage building into a honeymoon cottage. It was an aluminum building with no windows, but they didn't seem to mind.

The word got out Sunday morning that they had gotten married, and people from the opposing religion, along with a rejected lover, came to beat up the groom. I ran out just in time to lock the bride and groom in the storage building. In the meantime the Field Chairman came out just in time to stand between me and the angry crowd. He was a large man and could have a very stern face, so they were afraid of him. The rejected lover, however, put a curse on both the Field Chairman and me. Since it wasn't the first time some of the Mimika people had put a curse on me, we were just amused by it.

Then relief came. The parents of the bride were not in the village at the time, but they sent word that if anyone laid a hand on the newlyweds their corpse would be laid out in the front of the village. That did wonders to quieten things down.

BRIDE PRICE

Marriages were traditionally arranged by parents although that is changing some now and the young people have more say in who they will marry. The families get together and decide on the bride price. Every member of the bride's family including parents, brothers, uncles, etc. may say what they want. One thing that always amused me was that the mother of the bride always demanded "milk money." That was to reimburse her for nursing the bride when she was a baby. The groom never has enough resources to pay the price so ends up obligated for years to come to her family.

EATING SAGO

The Citak word for "to marry" was "to eat sago." The marriage consisted of both families getting together, and the bride price being paid. Afterward the bride would cook sago and serve the groom and his family. That was a sign of her commitment to her groom and his family, and from then on she had no more obligation to her own family, but became the "property" of the groom and his family. After all, they had paid for her. From then on every time she would go fishing or process sago she was expected to share it with her husband's family. She would be responsible to care for them in their old age.

When I first went there, I use to think that the ideal thing would be to have lots of daughters so they would generate the large bride prices. However, they wanted lots of boys to bring in lots of girls to take care of them. Social security Citak style.

GERSON AND PAULINA

Gerson lives in the village of Tamnim. His parents had already made arrangements with Paulina's parents and had settled on the bride price. However, Gerson had his eyes on Debet so was dragging his feet about marrying Paulina. This went on for quite some time.

Gerson was working with me on translating the Tamnim New Testament, so I followed the saga with much interest. He would tell me about the pressure being put on him by his parents as well as Paulina's parents. Yet he continued to stall.

After many weeks of this, one morning he came in to work and announced, "Nona, I got married last night." Of course, I was interested to know whom he had married.

He told this story. Paulina had become tired of waiting, picked up her machete, marched down the middle of the village to Gerson's house swinging her machete in his direction, demanding that he state his intentions. He was impressed at her insistence and said, "If you are so anxious to get married, then we will do it right now." They did.

I asked him if he was going to be satisfied with Paulina, since he had really wanted Debet and he answered, "Nona, the important thing is that *she* wants *me*."

Since the villagers all knew about his desire to have Debet, he felt that he should explain. Come Sunday he came up to the front of the church, along with his lovely barefoot bride, to give a testimony. Gerson said something like this, "I was married this week and my wife is standing here with me. I want all of you to understand why I married her. It was like this. It was like I had an old shirt that I didn't want anymore, so I threw it away and got a new one, and here she is." I looked around to see if the "old shirt" was in the service!

The next morning Gerson came to work all down in the mouth. He said that Debet's family was angry with him. I said, "About the shirt?" He seems sincerely confused as to why that would offend them I told him that he really should not have referred to Debet as an old shirt.

The next Sunday, he felt that he should get up once again and explain it. He should have left well enough alone. He said, "What I really meant was like this. It was like I had seen a pretty shirt in the kiosk and I really wanted it. However, the owner said that I couldn't have it, and besides it was too expensive, so I settled on a less desirable shirt!"

Yes, he came in again the next morning because his new wife and her family were all angry at him. I said, "Gerson, please don't mention that shirt anymore." I advised him to tell Debet and her family that she was a nice girl who would make some lucky man a good wife, but she just wasn't God's will for him.

I am happy to say that after several years and two children, Gerson and Paulina are in the process of living happily ever after.

FIRST CHURCH WEDDING AT SENGGO – TORKA AND TABITA

The Citak people had never had a church wedding before. Torka worked for me and they had arranged for him to marry Tabita and decided that this would be our very first "Christian" wedding. That is, Abdon decided to conduct the first Christian wedding.

You remember Abdon, don't you? He always had an opinion. Since he had never even seen a church wedding before, I assumed that he would want some help with it. However, he informed me that he knew just what to do and needed no help. "This should be interesting," I thought to myself.

They had the church all arranged with a short bench placed in front of the speaker's podium for Torka and Tabita. Torka was sitting on one side of the church with his face to the wall, while Tabita was sitting on the opposite side of the church facing that wall. I went back and brought them to their assigned seats. They both were very shy, and Torka sat on one end of the bench with his head down facing the west side of the church while Tabita sat on the other end facing the east side.

Abdon gave a charge to the bride and groom. His message went something like this, "In a family the husband and wife both have responsibilities. The husband's responsibility is to boss his wife. He is to tell her what to do. God made the man first and put him in charge. The wife's responsibility is to obey her husband and do whatever he tells her."

He held up his thumb and two fingers and said, "This represents the family. God is the tall one and is above them all. The next one is the husband right below God. The woman is the one down here." (pointing to his thumb). I was thinking, "Yeah, and just cut that thumb off and see where you would be."

Abdon then had the couple stand before him. They stood with their heads bowed too shy to lift them. Abdon said, "Torka, do you promise to boss your wife?" Torka answered, "Yeah." Then he said, "Tabita, do you promise to obey Torka? When he orders you to cut firewood, do you promise to do it? When he orders you to go get sago, do you promise to do it?" Tabita couldn't get a sound out, but mouthed, "Yeah." Abdon, "I pronounce you man and wife."

That was about 1980 and they are still living happily together with several children.

NIMROD RUMPOMBO

Nimrod was from the island of Biak on the north coast. After graduating from our Bible School there he moved to Amar to work with Marge and me. Nimrod was a very quiet humble man and a joy to work with. He started the church at Amar and was the pastor. He also built a school and taught it. He was a big help to Marge and me. He married a girl from the Mimika tribe at Amar.

Nimrod was a small man and his wife was rather large. In the Mimika culture, the wife was considered to be the possession of the husband, and he was expected to beat her for the first year to make her submissive. Nimrod had been taught in Bible School not to beat his wife. That made for a very interesting marriage.

Nimrod's wife was anything but submissive and did not submit to her own cultural norms. In fact, she was very different from any Mimika lady I had known. Turning tradition on its head, instead of Nimrod beating her, she would beat Nimrod on a regular basis. Her parents begged him to beat her. He would not. This continued for some time and, I became very impatient with it and called Nimrod in for a talk.

I definitely did NOT counsel him to beat his wife. However, I did tell him that he was wrong to allow his wife to beat him. A couple of nights after that, I heard a commotion down at his house and sneaked down in the dark to check it out. His wife was on the ground and he was standing over her with a stick in his hand. I smiled to myself and went home.

That happened a couple more times and then she settled down and they got along well together. I guess there really was something to beating your wife during the first year to beat her into submission! At least it worked for Nimrod.

Nimrod's wedding.

Chapter 21

PEOPLE I CAN'T FORGET

YOHANES

In this chapter I would like to introduce you to just a few of the individuals who stand out in my memory as being people who were very special to me.

Yohanes was from Kokonao in the Mimika tribe. His mother had died while he was still very small and his father gave him away. When he came to our school he was sick and frail, and evidently starving. We took him to live on the mission compound and began telling him of Christ.

The fear that is embedded in the people was very typical in Yohanes. Any strange sound or anything which looked different was, in his mind, caused by an evil spirit. He would not go outside at night because he believed that a spirit lived in the jungle behind our house, another one behind an out building, one in the tall grass in front of the house, and still another one in a strange looking tree down the trail a few hundred feet. Sometimes he was even afraid to go to sleep.

One day in class he began praying out loud, and asked Jesus to come into his heart. We talked with him and prayed, but the fear remained.

One day he asked about Heaven and we told him that Heaven was a beautiful place where there is no sorrow or hunger. He asked, "Is Satan there and can we walk outside at night?" When we told him that there was no night there, he wanted to go immediately.

Long ago, God sent angels with the message, "Fear not," and now He has given us the privilege of taking that same message to people who are bound by fear.

One day Yohanes climbed a coconut tree but forgot to take a machete. He began to cry. A man sent the machete up to him on a pole but Yohanes got stuck in the branches and dropped it. Then he couldn't get down out of the tree! He sat up there and cried for about 30 minutes while the whole community laughed. Finally, he got tired and came down.

About a year after that, Yohanes was diagnosed with tuberculosis, no doubt due to lack of sufficient food, plus the fact that he would allow the witch doctor to cut him with a razor blade and burn him with hot coals to chase away the evil spirits, yet would hide in the jungle to keep from getting shots.

Once we received a letter from my mother telling us that she was sending a package for Yohanes. We should not have told him right away because he thought that he would get it the next day. Packages normally took about a year to arrive. In order to help him understand, we cut a notch in the kitchen wall to show how tall he was then and then cut another notch to show how much he would have to grow before it came.

"But I'll be dead!" Yohanes said. He was both a challenge and a blessing to Marge and me. We will never forget him.

NIMROD RUMPUMBO–MARTYR FOR CHIRST

After I moved to Senggo, Nimrod, whom I mentioned in an earlier chapter, and his wife were moved to the village of Sumapero to minister along with Yonas Faidibon and his wife, Yohana. Sumapero was a very isolated village. Many of the Papuans were against the Indonesian government. They had formed a rebellion movement and were hiding out in the jungle near Sumapero.

Nimrod and Yonas had started a school and a church, and were busy teaching the people. Some outsiders came to the village. They thought that they had come from the government post to avoid the rebels. In fact, they *were* the rebels.

Yonas and Nimrod's wives welcomed them into their house and served them food and drink. They did not know just how wicked they were.

One morning the men were teaching in the school, never realizing that something bad was about to happen. At about 10:00 a.m. the rebels came to the school, chased the children outside and took the teachers hostage.

Then they forced the wives, along with Yohana's two children, to go with them into the jungle. They were treated badly and threatened with death.

After about two weeks, one morning Yonas went to the river for water to bathe their little girl. The rebels prevented him from returning, and also took Nimrod to the edge of the river. They tied the hands and feet of the two men, speared them to death, cut up their bodies and threw them into the river.

The women were taken into the jungle to be "wives" to the rebel leaders. Nimrod's wife, as you have already read, was large, aggressive, and knew the area. Yonas' wife was shy and did not know the area. Nimrod's wife managed to escape and return to Amar. Yohana remained hostage for the next 22 years.

Her story is related in detail in *"Hostage 22 Years in the Jungles of W. Papua, Indonesia"* by Yohana Faidibon with Dominggus Mayor. I had the privilege to translate the book into English. I encourage you to read that book. You will be blessed.

Nimrod and Yonas were martyrs in every sense of the word. They had graduated from Bible School and answered God's call to leave their homes and move to the south coast of the island to serve the Lord along with us. They were both humble men who had a desire to serve God, and they won the martyr's crown.

Nimrod

I am proud to have known them, and they are among the ones that I cannot forget.

TITUS FIAK

Here is a testimony by another memorable individual, Titus Fiak:

"As a small boy growing up in Irian Jaya, I heard from my father about headhunting raids he had gone on with others in our village. But government officials and a former missionary came to our village, and told the old people that they should stop practicing headhunting and cannibalism so I never participated in those things.

"The people in my village did not know about God. We thought that we just happened. We thought that when we died our spirits went into the jungle to be tested by the spirits of our ancestors. We would be given some food; and if we shared with the other spirits, we would be allowed to enter their village and live as spirits in the jungle. If we did not share the food, we would be sent into a hole in the ground forever and we would have to eat things such as maggots, worms and other bad stuff. We thought that everyone would go into the hole.

"From one of the first missionaries to our village I learned that God created us, that He loves us, and that His Son, Jesus, died for us. I learned that God had prepared a nice village for us to go to when we died. One day I decided that I wanted to follow God and become His child, so I confessed my sins to Him, and He forgave them.

"Eventually, those of us in the class who were Christians began to preach in the church services. The missionary would teach us a lesson, and one of us would teach it at church. After that missionary moved away, Margaret Stringer came and taught us more in our own language. One day she sent word to the village that she needed someone to help her learn our language. I had never had a job, but thought I might like helping her. So I volunteered myself, and I worked with her many years."

Titus worked with me for about 18 years. He was the primary one who helped me analyze and learn Citak, and then translate the New Testament. We worked together almost every morning during those years. Titus had been through six grades of schooling, and the New Testament never would have been translated without the help of Titus and others there.

It has been a great joy to see God take uneducated people living in a primitive culture, save them, fill them with His Spirit, and then use them in such a magnificent way.

The Citak wives were considered to be the property of the husband and they could beat them at will. We spent much time teaching them to love and respect their wives.

Titus genuinely loved his wife, Femasi. I never knew them to fight, and he never beat her. Not long before I came home Femasi became ill and after several weeks died. During all my time there I had never seen a man who sincerely mourned the death of his wife like Titus did. His example of a model husband was a testimony to everyone there. Titus is still at Senggo and I miss him so much. I grew to love him like a brother.

Titus Fiak

NOAK FIAK

It is difficult for me to write or think about Noak. He had a fourth grade education and could barely read. He had no formal Bible training other than the classes at Senggo, and was one of the first preachers in the church there. The medical staff trained him to be a village medical worker to treat the people.

Noak was such a blessing to teach. He would sit and soak up everything that he heard. We all considered him to be the most spiritual of all the Citak people at that time. He was our best, and had a great desire to serve the Lord. Once when we were talking, I told him that he would never be perfect until he got to Heaven. He cried because he wanted to be perfect right then.

Early photo of Noak

We placed Noak in the village of Komasma as their first evangelist/teacher/church planter. He taught Bible classes, men's Bible classes and Sunday services. He also dispensed medicines. Many people in that village were saved through his ministry there.

On a visit to Komasma I overheard Noak talking to some of the people. He said, "Somebody gave the gospel to Nona Margaret. She left her home and came here, learned our language and told us at Senggo. Now we are here teaching you. When you understand, you should go to another village and tell them. Then they will go on to yet another village, and in that way everybody can hear." That expressed it very nicely, didn't it?

I loved Noak – and still do. He was very much involved in entering the villages along the Brazza River. The people there were still killing and eating their enemies. They loved Noak and called him "Ndoak." He was one of the two men with me when we made the first trip into the village of Vakabuis, about which you can read in my book, *"From Cannibalism to Christianity."*

Later we placed him in one of the Brazza area villages, which were steeped in heathenism. Noak was our best. We put our best in the place where Satan had always had full control. However, after some time there Noak began to act a bit strange and paranoid. Over a period of time he became psychotic.

In the beginning he told me that someone in the village had put a curse on him. He was told that he would drown. Normally, if a Citak person felt that a curse had been put on him and was told that he would drown, he would just fall into the water and drown. Noak defied the curse. I had never seen anyone do that before, and was so very proud of him.

One day Noak was out in his canoe fishing when his fishhook got caught on a log on the bottom of the river. The normal thing to do feeling that a curse had been put on him would be to dive into the water and drown. He defied the curse, dived into the water, and rescued his fishhook. I saw that as a real miracle.

However, I was disappointed to see him continue to deteriorate. Then he believed that a man from our Indonesian language church had put a curse on him. That man was from the island of Biak off the northwest coast of the island.

Here I will copy part of the chapter out of my book mentioned above:

"There were several Biak families at Senggo who were all in the Indonesian language church. Noak became extremely paranoid and developed a deep hatred of all Biak people. He felt that if he killed one of them, then the curse would be lifted off him. One day in late 1992, Mr. Yensenem, a Biak man, was visiting in the village at Senggo when Noak sneaked up behind him with a hatchet. He jumped out suddenly and split Mr. Yensenem's head open. The hatchet went through his skull and into his brain.

"Noak was not necessarily angry with Yensenem; his only fault was that he was a Biakker. This unwarranted attack set off many angry reactions and threats of retaliation towards Noak's relatives, mainly Titus Fiak, my main translation helper and pastor of the Citak language church; and Abdon Fiak.

"Titus' wife was Noak's sister. This situation threatened to become an all-out war between the Indonesian language church people and the Citak language church, as their old culture of revenge resurfaced.

"The translation ministry almost came to a halt as my primary helpers were in hiding. Other church activities either stopped or were poorly attended as the people were afraid. Several confrontations almost ended in bloodshed. One time the people got their spears and bows and arrows and prepared to go to war until someone said, "We have left that, and we are following the Lord!" They put down their weapons. Needless to say, this was a very difficult time for all of us. All of the people on both sides of the issue were Christians from the Indonesian and Citak language churches.

"Yensenem was in a coma for several weeks while his fellow Biakkers waited for him to regain consciousness and tell them what to do. It was a very tense time as Yensenem's two sons were very angry and making serious threats. As a result, many of the Fiak clan stayed hidden in the jungle. When Yensenem finally regained consciousness, the first thing he said was for them not to retaliate. His attitude has been great as he demonstrated the presence of God in his heart and life. He remains paralyzed on one side from the injury to his brain.

"Our hearts grieved for both Yensenem and Noak. Noak was arrested and locked in a windowless room there at Senggo. Ruth and I visited him and hoped to see some sign of remorse. Remembering how he had wanted to be perfect for God, we asked him what he thought about all day in that room. He said, "I think about how hot it is in that room with no windows." Sad to say, he showed no sign of remorse.

"They sent him out to the capital to the very inefficient psychiatric hospital. When they brought him to the airstrip to leave Senggo, he looked so pitiful walking along in handcuffs looking a bit frightened but also a bit proud. The Senggo people mourned, and I mourned with them in my heart.

"Eventually, apologies were made between Yensenem and Titus and Abdon, and relations between the churches began to return to normal.

"However, Noak continued to deteriorate and became more determined in his efforts to kill a Biak person. He was eventually returned to Senggo, and he terrorized everyone there. He began directing his anger not only at the Biak people, but also toward his own people. I talked with him just before leaving for furlough and said, "Noak, I fear that you will kill someone, and then you will be killed." He said, "That is what I want."

Shortly after arriving in the U.S. for furlough I received this news:

"One night while carrying his weapons – a spear and a knife, he began stalking the house of a Biak family. A young man from the neighboring Asmat tribe who had come to Senggo for medicine didn't know the situation with Noak, and decided to be a hero and hold Noak. All the people were afraid to come out of their houses, and the young man was found dead the next morning."

Noak is still at Senggo, and there have been frequent incidents where he has threatened someone else. We have to have police guarding when we have a special service at night for the Indonesian congregation. His weapons have all been confiscated and his wife is staying in another house out of fear for her own life. Noak doesn't want to hear the name of God and becomes angry if it is mentioned.

I left Senggo in October, 2004.

The following is copied from by book, *"From Cannibalism to Christianity"*:

"In the 40-plus years I spent in Papua this was no doubt most disappointing experience. I loved Noak, and still do. I continue to claim him for the Lord. Satan has obviously won a battle, but I believe that God will win that war in the end."

LATEST NEWS ABOUT NOAK FIAK

Noak continued to terrorize everyone around him and often made threats. Many people prayed regularly for Noak, but it appeared that he would never get any better. I was convinced that Noak was a Christian, although I could not understand what had happened to him. I am absolutely certain that I will see the old Noak when we get to heaven.

In 2011, Gail Vinje had been diagnosed with pancreatic cancer and we went to Papua to pack up her things. Noak got the word about her cancer and came to the house. As Gail explained her situation to him, he very gently placed his hand on her abdomen and looked at her with real concern. I had not seen that look in years.

The people told us that Noak had really changed. He no longer tried to kill people, was friendly and generous with the children, and often gave them money. He visited in the homes of the villagers and seemed much calmer. He appeared normal.

Kris, the pastor of the Citak church, told me that Noak had come to him one day carrying a knife and ordered Kris to pray for him. Normally, if anyone saw Noak holding any kind of weapon they would run away. Kris told him to lay down his knife, and to come into the house. Noak refused to lay his knife down, and told Kris that he would stab him with it if he did not pray for him. Kris motioned for his wife and children to run out the back door, and invited Noak in. They sat down face to face, and Noak laid the knife down beside him. Kris placed his hand on Noak's head and began to pray.

Kris said, "Nona, I don't know what happened, but while I was praying, my hand jumped up. I didn't do anything and Noak didn't do anything, but it jumped up off Noak's head all by itself." Noak has been different ever since then; not completely back to the old Noak, but changed.

Normally, if Noak was seen coming towards the church everyone would run away. That Sunday when Gail and I were there, Noak came walking to church carrying his Bible. That had not happened for many years. After the service, he stood around and talked with several people. No one seemed to be afraid.

As I write this, it is May, 2014. One of our former missionaries just returned from a visit to Papua and Senggo. Noak's daughter reported, "Noak is better. He is not like he used to be." However, she is concerned that Noak has begun to smoke.

We know that God is able to completely heal Noak. His problem could be the result of the involvement of evil spirits in his life, or perhaps schizophrenia. Regardless of the cause, God is greater than either of them, so we continue to pray that He will intervene in Noak's life until he returns to become an even greater vessel for God than he was before.

Noak was perhaps my greatest disappointment in the ministry, yet at the same time one of my greatest joys in the beginning. God gave me a real love for Noak. I can never forget him.

Noak in 2011

KRIS BAGASU

This is a good place to introduce you to Kris Bagasu. He was just a little boy when I first got to know him when he attended the class I had for the Citak children. He seldom missed a class, listened intently, memorized the verses, but hardly ever said a word.

He finished sixth grade in school and would have had to leave the area in order to continue his education. I wanted him to go to Bible School but he preferred to get married instead. He married my namesake, Margareta.

Kris was growing spiritually and was very active in the church. Titus was slowing down, and I began looking for someone to work with us on a full-time basis. I asked

Kris to come to work. He worked for several years along with Titus in completing the translation of the New Testament. It was a joy to work with him. He became the pastor of the Citak church after Titus retired. After several years he still remains in that position, and is a tremendous joy and blessing.

The leadership of the National Church Organization wanted to ordain Kris. He came to me saying, "I don't think I should be ordained because I have not been to Bible School." I reminded him that he had been through every verse in the New Testament several times, delving deeply into the meaning of every word. We had also translated many Old Testament stories. He no doubt had a greater knowledge of Scripture than most people Bible school graduates.

Kris was examined by the Ordination Committee, and one of the members told me that he did better than anyone he had ever examined. I was so very proud of him.

We tried for years to teach the people the importance of supporting their pastor, but with little progress. The last time I was there, in 2011, Kris said, "Nona, they are helping me a little. Some people give me fish, and some have given me money. It doesn't matter, though. Whether they support me or not, I will serve the Lord until I die."

Kris has always been so happy about having the New Testament and every time I have been back he has repeated, "Thank you for translating the Bible for us. It is my guide for life."

Before I came home, Kris' little boy, Yunus, declared that he would go to school only if he had shoes and a book satchel. Since nobody else in first grade had either of these things we didn't feel it was necessary that Yunus have them, so I made him a promise. I told him, "If you go to school and graduate from sixth grade, I will buy shoes and a book satchel for you."

Then I came home and forgot my promise. Yunus, however, did not forget. Gail was at Merauke at the time, and Yunus got word to Gail to send word to me that he had graduated from sixth grade and wanted his shoes and book satchel. Of course, I sent funds to Gail with instructions to get good shoes and a really nice satchel for my "grandson" Yunus.

Kris and his family are people whom I definitely cannot forget.

Kris Bagasu and family. Yunus is the tallest boy.

SEDO VAKABUIS

The first time I saw Sedo was in September 1980, when we swung out of the helicopter in the village of Vakabuis into the waiting arms of wildly dancing naked men. Sedo was obvious because he was larger than most everyone else.

Another thing that was obvious about Sedo was his smile. He was always friendly, and I never saw him without his big smile. Looks, however, can be deceiving.

169

He was the assistant chief of his clan, a position he had achieved by killing and helping to eat three men. He loved to show off his wounds from a war where an enemy arrow went through his thigh.

Sedo had three wives, two of whom had been stolen on raids on enemy clans. Once when we were visiting the village of Vakabuis, Sedo told me with a big smile that one of his wives had run away into the jungle. When I asked why, he said, "She is afraid of me because I beat her."

Shortly after that we learned that he had gotten angry at her, chased her into the jungle, killed her with his bow and arrow and left her body to rot in the jungle.

When the Vakabuis people threatened the lives of Gail Vinje and me in 1983, Sedo was not involved. He always gave us a good welcome and always seemed happy to see us. He had heard the gospel and, although he listened, he showed little interest. Later, word came to us that Sedo had died. We were saddened by the news. I was sad because he was a friend, but even more so because he went into eternity without Christ.

Sedo Vakabuis

BOAR ESAUN

Boar was the chief of the village of Esaun. He achieved that position of leadership by killing and helping to eat three men. I met him shortly after that first visit to Vakabuis. The village of Esaun was close to Vakabuis, and we had made contact with them on subsequent trips.

When the lives of Gail and me were threatened, Boar was visiting Vakabuis and was probably one of the main agitators against us. He had heard the gospel from various sources, the main one being Oto Arenu, the evangelist sent by the Senggo church to his village. Oto and Paulina Arenu had moved from Tamnim near Senggo to Esaun to teach them. After they had been there for several months I went up for a visit.

In the evening we sat around with the people in their huts, talking and visiting with them. Sedo at Vakabuis had recently died and we were talking about him. Boar said, "Sedo never did ask God to forgive his sins, did he?"

"No," I answered.

Boar asked, "He went to hell, didn't he?"

"Yes," I said.

"Can I confess my sins to God and ask him to forgive me?" he asked.

"Of course," I replied.

Boar prayed and asked God to forgive him. After he finished, I asked him, "Boar, who is your father now?"

He thought for a while and said, "God is my father."

I said, "God is also my father. What does that make us?"

After thinking a bit he smiled and answered, "We are brother and sister."

171

Boar Esaun

Boar, who had killed and eaten people, and who had threatened to kill Gail and me, had become our brother. Praise the Lord for His amazing grace.

Sometime afterward a group from the village of Bubis/ Esaun were at Senggo and came to a service. The villages of Bubis and Esaun had merged into one village. They had just held their first baptismal service a couple of months before. Boar, along with two other war chiefs from the village, surprised us by running in during the singing all dressed out with war paint and carrying bows and arrows.

They danced around in front of the audience, chanting like only the Citak people can do, depicting a war dance. Then they said, "We used to be headhunters and ate the flesh of our enemies. Then the gospel came to our village and we accepted Christ as our Savior and have stopped warring and eating people. We were baptized last month and as a token of our decision to follow the Lord, we want to present our bows and arrows to the missionary, the church and the government." Then one of them came and presented his bows and arrows to me. It was a thrilling experience.

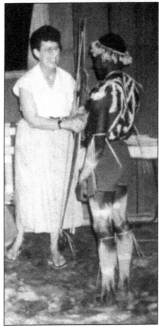

Presenting weapons

Just before I came home to retire in November 2004 we had helped the people at Bubis/Esaun build a church. Several of us went up to dedicate the church and it was a thrill to watch Boar sitting right up front worshiping the Lord. We came out and were preparing to get in the boat to return to Senggo when he came over to me and said, "Nona, thank you for coming. Thank you for telling us how we can go to heaven. You brought us out of darkness into the light."

Every sacrifice and hardship was forgotten at that moment, and I thanked God for allowing me the joy of knowing Boar. He is still there and I am so proud that he is my brother. You may read more about Boar in my book, *"From Cannibalism to Christianity."*

Boar Esaun in 2004

PEMAR AND TURBIS BAGASU

When I first went to Senggo, Pemar became my new best friend. If someone came to my house and said, "Your friend is sick," I knew that it was Pemar. She was married to probably the most powerful witch doctor at Senggo, a man named Turbis. He was no doubt the most feared man in the village.

I was visiting one day with Pemar and Toro, and they told me about how they used to fight and eat the flesh of their enemies and how they danced and sang at the victory feast. I asked her where her spirit would go when she died.

Pemar replied, "To the evil spirit village, but that is bad. Perhaps your spirit will be a good one but mine will be a bad one." She went on to say that she would like to go to "that Man-up-there's" village. What a thrill it was to tell her that she could indeed go to "that Man-up-there's" village. She was the first lady at Senggo to become a Christian.

Pemar exercised great patience in trying to help me learn her language and I spent many afternoon hours in her house "talking." Sometimes I would go with her into the jungle to search for food, such as sago and fish.

When I started the literacy class, Pemar was one of my students. She had never held a pencil or a book, but she was excited to learn. She went home after the first class, proudly clutching her pretty yellow book.

Later that afternoon someone came running to my house saying, "Turbis beat your friend because she had come to your class." Apparently he was embarrassed that she had come home with a book that she could not read. I thought, "Am I brave enough to confront the witch doctor?" I prayed and mustered up my courage and went down to the village.

When I arrived, the villagers were standing around expectantly. Someone asked, "Are you going to talk to Turbis?"

I said a bit weakly, "Yes." When I entered the house Turbis was sitting on the floor near the fire cooking sago. Pemar was sitting a short distance away. He had beaten her badly with a stick of firewood.

I prayed again silently and confronted Turbis, who had not even acknowledged my presence. I said, "Turbis, you know that Pemar is my friend, and I feel really bad that you beat her. I feel that it is my fault since you were angry that she had come to my class."

He ignored me completely and continued to cook his sago. I finally decided that I would get nowhere with him, so I talked a bit with Pemar, checked her injuries, and then stood up to leave. As I started toward the door Turbis said, "Nona."

I turned back, and he was holding out a piece of sago to me. Here is an example of how important it is to know the customs of the people. I knew that if someone had offended another person and wanted to apologize, in order to do so they would offer the offended person some food. If they accepted the food, it meant that they had accepted the "apology."

I came back, sat down and took the sago. While I was eating it Turbis said, "I am sorry that I beat Pemar."

I thought, "Apologize to *her!*"

When I went outside, the villagers standing around asked, "Did you eat sago with Turbis?"

"Of course," I proudly announced.

I am so happy to report that several months later Turbis also became my brother! Their son, Bernard, was the first person from the Citak tribe to go away to Bible School. He is at Senggo now working in the church. Pemar later became ill and wasted away to just skin and bones. and was awful to look at. In August 1992 she went to be with the Lord.

I came home at the end of 2004 and returned for a visit in 2008. Turbis met me on the path from the airstrip to my house, and apologized for not meeting me at the airplane because he was sick.

After settling in, I went down to visit Turbis and he indeed was very sick. The next day some of the people came to tell me that he had died. When a person dies, the people mourn all day and bury him the same day. I stayed with them all day as we mourned the death of my friend, Turbis. As I was sitting with the people I thought, "Before he became a Christian, everybody feared Turbis. When he died nobody was afraid of him."

It was a privilege to have known Pemar and Turbis, my friends.

Pemar and Turbis

YOS ONDI

Yos was not a Citakker. He came to Senggo from the town of Sentani on the north coast of the island. He had led a pretty rough life. His father had died when he was a baby, and when he was six years old he awoke one morning in the arms of his dead mother. Different family members took care of him and he graduated from sixth grade.

He learned to work in construction and other things. As a teen he formed a gang and they burglarized stores for money. He also worked for a while for the Indonesian government to keep eyes on the Dutch, as the Indonesians were preparing to take over what was then Dutch New Guinea.

When he was 17 years old he met Klasina. They were married in 1963. Later he joined the Indonesian army, and since they gave him a gun, he used it to get what he wanted. He did not fully agree with the Indonesians and managed to get out of the army. Then he was accused of rebelling against the government, and was arrested and sentenced to be executed by hanging.

Klasina was a Christian and witnessed to him to no avail. Then came the day for his execution, and the noose was placed around his neck. Just before losing consciousness, he confessed his sin and received Christ as his Savior.

The trap door opened and Yos fell through. He opened his eyes to see people standing over him. The rope had broken, and he was lying on the ground beneath the gallows. Yos knew at that moment that the Lord had spared him for a purpose. The army was afraid to try to hang him again because they also felt that he had escaped death by a miracle. He remained in prison for another year, and when he was released, he prayed that the Lord would give him something to do for Him.

The missionaries at that time were in the process of opening the work at Senggo. They had heard about Yos and about his skill as a construction worker and he was invited to come to Senggo to help build the hospital.

In 1974 Yos felt that God was calling him to leave his home and move several hundred miles away to the jungle at Senggo. In 1975 Klasina left a good job in Sentani and moved to Senggo with him. They are still there. I cannot say enough about the blessing that Yos and Klasina Ondy have been to everyone at Senggo. It is impossible for us to visualize the rough man that he once was. He is one of the most humble men I have ever known.

Yos did not preach, but did just about everything else. He came as a carpenter, but became one of the main leaders in the Indonesian language church. Both he and Klasina were active in every part of the ministry, especially in the Indonesian speaking community.

Yos was one of several men who operated the outboard motor. I got to spend many hours on the rivers with him as we visited the outlying villages.

I cannot forget the Ondys.

Yos Ondy family

SIPRIANUS WAMBRAU

Siprianus also was not a Citakker, but was from the small island of Biak, which is located off the northwest coast of Papua. He was a graduate of our Bible School near there, and the Lord led him to come with his family to work with us at Senggo. He was already there when I arrived, so we were together in the ministry there for almost 30 years.

Siprianus was one of the primary church leaders in the Indonesian language church. My main association with Siprianus was that he operated the outboard motor, taking myself and others to the outlying villages. We spent many hours and days together on the jungle rivers, sleeping in the native huts, talking and laughing a lot.

He loved to work! He made every effort to make the trips as comfortable as possible for me, especially after I broke by back and didn't travel as well as before. He would go down to the boat house early and prepare the boat and my seat.

One thing I remember especially about Siprianus was when one of his sons announced that he was ready to marry. He asked his father to return to Biak and find a wife for him, stating that he would be happy with whomever his father picked.

Siprianus flew out of Senggo and headed to Biak to find a wife for his son. I called him Eliezer. We all gathered beside the airstrip when he returned as we all wanted to see her. She was lovely and very young. We immediately worried that she would get homesick, and cry to return to her home. She kept glancing at him and he kept glancing at her, and it was love at first sight.

We had a big wedding for them and she never showed any sign of being homesick. It was amazing how quickly she matured. They are still at Senggo, doing great, and at last count they had four children.

I love Siprianus and his wife and family.

Siprianus Wambrau

DOMINGGUS MAYOR

Last, but certainly not least, is Dominggus Mayor. He also was from Biak and a graduate of our Bible School. He brought his family to the South Coast to work with our doctor and his wife, Ken and Sylvia Dresser. Dominggus and his family had come to the South Coast about the same time as when I arrived on the field. They did not keep birth records, so he did not know how old he was, but we figured that we were about the same age. We often said that we had grown up together since we both were young when we first met.

Dominggus was the main leader of the Indonesian language church, and was also one who often operated the outboard motor on village trips. We became very close friends, and it was easy to think of Dominggus as a brother.

I remember once when we went to a village for a church dedication. We stayed with the native teacher there so the accommodations were a bit better than the village huts. The teacher showed me my very own room, which they had completely cleaned out. I felt honored by their consideration since many times I had slept in the same room with everybody else. I hung my mosquito net, put down my sleeping bag, and went to bed.

When I woke up around daylight and looked across the room, lo and behold, there was Dominggus. They had given him the same room! He had very graciously waited until I had gone to sleep to sneak in.

It was not odd for all of us to sleep together in one room when we went to the outlying villages because the native huts had only one room, so the teacher did not think it a problem at all to put us both in the same room.

You may read about Dominggus in *"From Cannibalism to Christianity."* He, along with Noak, were with me on that first exciting trip to Vakabuis. When Gail and I had to be evacuated, it was Dominggus who came up the river to meet us to take us back to Senggo. He retired and returned to Biak, where he started a church. His wife died after I came home, but Dominggus is still there.

I can't express the love and respect I have for Dominggus.

Dominggus Mayor

There are many more people whom I cannot forget who added so much to my life and I wish that I could have told you about all of them. I look forward to heaven where I can introduce them all to you, and where I can fellowship with them, my brothers and sisters, forever.

Chapter 22

PERFECT LOVE
CASTETH OUT FEAR

"Oh, please, may I go in the airplane to your country?" The expression on the man's face was one of dread and fear, and his eyes were pleading for help. We sensed that something terrible was wrong not only from his face, but because we knew that only real fear would bring him out this late at night. When asked what was wrong, he told about how a few days before, the men in the village had gone into the jungle on a pig hunt. This man somehow became separated from the rest and was lost in the jungle for two days before being found.

Everyone seemed happy to see him until this night when his family and the entire village threw him out with nowhere to go, and without a friend in the world other than the missionaries. Their reason for this action was because "He got evil spirits in the jungle."

Once, over the period of just a few days several young healthy men died. They feared that a curse had been put on them.

A Christian young man from Senggo was obviously dying but it was just as obvious that he had no medical reason for it. He said that someone had put a curse on him and that the spirits had told him that he would die in three days. We stayed with him around the clock talking with him and praying. He told his family what to do after his death, and in spite of everything we did, on the third day, he died.

When I first began to teach about the evil spirits it would terrify them just to hear me say the word. They would not say the word themselves.

We can never really understand their fear, but it was real. We could teach them, however, that God is greater than any spirit, and He can calm any fear by trusting in Him.

Matthew 10:31 *"Fear ye not therefore, ye are of more value than many sparrows."*

2 Timothy 1:7 *"For God hath not given us the spirit of fear; but of power, and of love, and of a sound mind."*

1 John 4:18 *There is no fear in love; but perfect love casteth out fear: because fear hath torment. He that feareth is not made perfect in love."*

Fear indeed did cause much torment for the Citak people, and it was just one of the joys of living and ministering in the Citak tribe to watch them come to trust the Lord, and slowly begin to lose their fear of the evil spirits.

We had the thrill of watching the "witch doctors" either become Christians or simply to give up their practice. That was due to biblical teaching, and largely to the loving medical help and teaching that was being given to them by the medical staff at Senggo. It did not take them long to figure out that the medicine given to them was far superior to what the witch doctors had been doing.

FETISH BURNING

One day the church leader at the village of Tamnim came to me and said that they wanted to have a "fetish burning" service. That confused me as they did not have fetishes. If one wanted to put a curse on someone they would simply get a small stick, say a chant over it, and lay it down in front of the house of the one on whom they were putting the curse. When that person stepped over the stick, the curse was on him.

A small piece of paper dropped on the soccer field could cause a major fight because they believed that someone had said the chant on the paper in order to curse the opposing team.

Saying a chant over a small stick and putting it in the arrow would help them to shoot animals. So how can you burn a chant?

Since this was all their idea, we decided just to watch to see what they had come up with. We gathered at the church where they had small pieces of paper laying on a bench in front of the church. The people came up one at a time, picked up one of the pieces of paper, held it up and told what kind of witch craft they had been using and made a vow not to use it anymore. Then they laid the paper down on the dirt floor.

Some confessed that they had stopped practicing witch craft after becoming a Christian and made a vow not to use it again. Then they burned the pieces of paper.

Fetish burning

Kosmos' confession really impressed me. I had fool-ishly attempted to get the people to tell me what they said in the chants. No one would tell me, and finally I had given up trying. Kosmos said, "I have not used witchcraft since becoming a Christian, but the chant keeps going over and over in my mind."

I thanked God that nobody would tell me those chants. Also, the implications of that struck me. A fetish that people in other tribes wore around their necks could be burned, and it would be over with, but something in the mind could not be as easily disposed of. We realized that we needed to pray that the Holy Spirit would control their minds.

This spread to some of the outlying villages and they also had "fetish" burnings. It thrilled us because that was something that they themselves decided needed to be done.

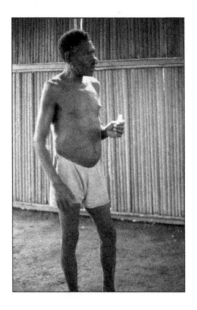

Fetish burning

Perfect love does indeed cast out fear, and God the Holy Spirit revealed His perfect love to them and then they could live without the fear that had held them hostage from the beginning.

Chapter 23

MEMORABLE CHURCH SERVICES/CLASSES

Dogs, chickens, and sometimes pigs, were some of our most faithful attendees at church. There was hardly a service without dogs. Ruth had a large dog who loved to attend my children's classes. Sometimes he disturbed the class, so, I decided one day to keep him out. After all the children had come in, I carefully closed the front door. The church had a dirt floor and dogs, and other animals, had dug out the dirt under the side door. But, that didn't concern me, as I figured that Ruth's dog was too large for that hole.

About 50 children gathered and I began the class – free of the dog. What I did NOT know was, that the dog had already come in, before I closed the door, and was sleeping under a bench toward the back of the church. He was closed IN, not OUT. About the time that I reached the best part of the lesson, a chicken with all her little chicks strolled into the church through the hole under the side door. I intended to quietly shoo her back through the hole, but just at that moment the dog woke up! Total bedlam broke out. The dog started barking and chasing chickens. Chickens were flying all over the place. I was screaming for the kids to open the doors. Needless to say, the kids were delighted with all the excitement.

In the more sophisticated Indonesian language service, the song leader led us to sing a chorus in a round, but he kept starting off the second group at the wrong time and it sounded like a bunch of people talking in tongues. He finally motioned for us to stop, but several women didn't see him and screeched out the next words by themselves.

The men sat on one side of the church and the women on the other. Several of the women, including me, giggled out loud. One of the men across the aisle yelled, "SHUT UP OVER THERE! DON'T YOU KNOW YOU ARE IN GOD'S HOUSE? YOU ARE SUPPOSED TO SIT QUIETLY IN GOD'S HOUSE! SO SHUT UP THAT LAUGHING! WHAT DO YOU MEAN, SITTING AND LAUGHING IN GOD'S HOUSE?" By then, there was no way I could stop laughing. I have a feeling that God enjoyed our laughing much more than the man's angry outburst.

One Sunday morning, we found a snake sleeping on one of the benches. The men are as afraid of snakes as I am, and they ran around screaming and yelling, and nobody seemed to have enough courage to get rid of it. They decided unanimously not to kill it, because it was not poisonous. Some wanted to just let it sleep as it didn't seem inclined to move. Also, I didn't feel inclined to stay for church. There were others also, who refused to worship with a snake – poisonous or not. Finally, a lady with a look of pure disgust at the rest of us walked up nonchalantly, with a small stick in her hand. She broke it in two, used one to nudge the snake to wrap itself around the other one and calmly took it out and threw it away. What courage!

I eventually got so used to all the animals in church that I hardly even noticed them. That is, unless a pig came waltzing in and a lady picked it up to take it out, and it didn't want to go, and squealed all the way. It was hard not to notice that.

One Sunday morning, a young man came in proudly wearing his very first pair of shoes–bulky tennis shoes. He strutted up to take up the offering. When he came down the aisle with it, he stepped on his shoe string, fell flat on his face, and slung the offering down the aisle. He got up, gathered up the offering, started out again, and did the same thing again.

This fiasco was a prime example of what God says in His word, that "Pride goeth before a fall."

Chapter 24

MAYBE ROME WASN'T BUILT IN A DAY, BUT THE ABAU CHURCH WAS!

I was spending some time in the Citak village of Abau. Ben Abau, the church leader came and expressed his concern that they had no place to hold Sunday services. (It's called planning ahead.) "But, we'll build one tomorrow." he said, Feeling a bit skeptical, I awoke at 5:30 the next morning to hear Ben shouting out the assignments. Some of the men were to cut wood for the frame, others for the benches, and still others for the half walls. Each of the women were to bring eight sections of thatched roofing, woven from palm leaves.

Not wishing to shirk my responsibility as a village dweller, I gave it a try. However, after struggling to finish one section while the woman next to me did four, I think it was to everyone's relief – especially mine – that I gave up when I did. In fact, I hoped that I would not be sitting under my section if it rained. For the next several days, I picked out small thorns that had buried themselves in my hand, as I had worked with the large prickly leaves.

Work progressed steadily throughout the day. They had no nails so they used vines to tie the framework together and to secure the thatched roofing. Long pieces of wood were fixed on notched poles planted in the ground to serve as benches. The finishing touches were added and by dark the building was completed.

At last, having missed lunch, we sat down around the fire to indulge in our long-awaited supper of fish and sago. Our peaceful fireside meal was interrupted by the village "crier" bellowing out his announcement, as he urged everyone to gather to dance as a means of celebrating their day's achievement. Since that dance frequently resulted in immorality among its participants, I quickly suggested to Ben that the people gather at the church instead for a praise service. I explained that it would be a great disappointment to have them serve the Lord all day in building the church, and then fail Him in their celebration. Everyone agreed, so we took the lantern, the cassette player, and cassettes of Citak songs, and enjoyed a time of praise in the new church building.

Admittedly, the "First Church at Abau" did not quite compare to the average "First Church of USAville," but it served the same purpose – providing a place for Christians to gather and worship the Lord and to hear from His Word. And it was all built in a day!

Abau village church

There were 20 outlying villages, in addition to Senggo and Tamnim. They all eventually had some kind of church building. Most of them, like the Abau church, were built with native materials, and as they did not last long, they had to be rebuilt every few years.

Occasionally, some of the men from Senggo would go to the villages to help the people of those villages lay out their church buildings. They could not figure out what size church they needed, and as a result, they would either build it large enough for triple the number of people in the village, or else way too small.

I remember the church at Komasma in particular. It was very narrow and very long. Normally, ladies would sit on one side, with the men on the other. The church was not wide enough for that particular seating arrangement, so the men sat in front and the ladies in back. I doubt if they were able to hear much of the service.

Noak was ministering there when Titus and I went for a visit. Noak had done a great job of teaching them, but sometimes there are things that don't come across well. The ladies obviously had not heard everything that had been taught. It was Sunday morning and Titus preached a good message and then gave an invitation. Forty people indicated a desire to be saved. Titus dealt with the men at the front of the church, and I went to the back of the church to deal with the ladies. As usual, I started with inviting them to admit their sin. I had never had anyone to deny that they had ever sinned – but those ladies did. It went something like this: I said, "Would all of you who have ever sinned, please raise your hands." Not one hand was raised. They all sat with their heads bowed. I began to ask individuals, "Have you ever sinned?"

"No."

"Have you ever stolen anyone's fish off their fish line?"

"No."

"Have you ever put a curse on anyone?"

"No."

"Have you ever had a fight with anyone?"

"No."

On and on it went and not a one would admit to sinning. Then I asked, "Why did you raise your hands?"

"Because we want to go to heaven," one lady answered.

I thought, "Then I guess you are all going since none of you have ever sinned."

By then I began to wonder about the men, so I marched the ladies up to the front of the church and interrupted Titus as he was dealing with the men. I told him that the ladies thought that they had never sinned and perhaps the men had also misunderstood something. Titus asked the men, "Have you sinned?" Every one of them raised their hands. He then told them, "The women say that they have never sinned."

I wish you could have been there. Husbands and other male family members began laughing and ridiculing the women and confessing their sins for them. "You were mad at me just this morning." "I saw you steal a fish yesterday afternoon." "You two had a fight today."

The women sat with their heads bowed as Titus asked them, "Did you do all of that?"

"Yes," they humbly answered.

Titus looked at me as if to say, "What is the matter with you? They are admitting that they are sinners." Yeah, with a little help from the men.

I marched them to the rear of the church, and with great joy told them that it was not by denying their sin, but by admitting it that they could go to heaven. They had understood enough to know that no sin could go to heaven. They thought that Titus and I had come to Komasma to declare which of them could go to heaven, and that if they admitted that they had sinned, then *we* would not allow them to go to heaven. They seemed relieved that neither Titus nor I would be making that decision. They happily confessed their sins to God and asked Him to save them. We then encouraged the people to rearrange the seating in the church so that the ladies could hear the sermons.

Following are some of the village churches.

Village churches

Chapter 25

CHRISTMAS AT SENGGO

We began to celebrate Christmas and Easter. In the beginning they could not remember if we were celebrating Jesus' birth, His death, or His resurrection. The children's Christmas parties were always fun and memorable. The first year that we gave gifts was exciting. I brought used wrapping paper back with me from furlough, and all the missionaries at Senggo had saved their toilet paper rolls.

We put several pieces of hard candy inside them and wrapped them with the used paper, tying the ends. Seeing the excitement of the children over several pieces of hard candy in a toilet paper roll would embarrass any of us when we think of what we waste at Christmas. The children came running out of the church waving their gifts, screaming and dancing, just as if they had received something very nice and expensive.

When I went back for a visit in 2008, we had a Christmas party for them and gave them Ziploc bags full of pencils, sparklers, candy, toys, etc. Their joyful reaction was the same as when they rejoiced over their "big" Christmas gifts. We always told them that the gifts were just a small token to remind them of the greatest gift of all – Jesus Christ. We never ceased to rejoice over the joy we experienced in telling them that Good News.

As I promised in a previous chapter, following is my debut as a drama producer – and I decided that it would be my last.

The people were learning what Christmas was when I planned to dramatize it. What I had not taken into account was that I knew very little about producing a play, and that the people knew nothing about acting. They absolutely would not act. When I would tell them what to say, they repeated it in the same monotone voice that I had used. They seemed not to have any idea what was going on. Not to be discouraged, I kept at it.

I strung a wire across the front of the church and made curtains with some old curtains I had, and hung them with the flip-up tabs from empty soda cans that I had brought back from furlough. I borrowed house coats from everyone on the station, for the shepherds and wise men. We didn't have enough, so the shepherds were to come in the front of the church and find the baby in the manger. Then, they were supposed to take off their robes and give them to the wise men. The shepherds came in and worshiped the baby. Then the time came for the wise men to come in, but they did not come in. I ran around the church to send them in, but they were not there. I came running back like a wild lady hunting for them.

Someone said, "There they are, Nona." They had been right there sitting near me all the time.

I asked, "Why are you not out there coming in?"

"We don't have any robes," they said.

"Where are the robes?" I asked

"The shepherds are still wearing them," they replied.

The shepherds were sitting calmly nearby as if nothing was happening. I asked, not too kindly, "Why didn't you give the robes to the wise men?"

"You didn't tell us to," they answered. I declared that I would never try that again.

The next year they came to me asking if they could do another Christmas play. I answered, "Yes, *you* may put on a Christmas play, but *you* must do it." They asked if they could do the death of Christ instead of His birth and I said, of course, since He was born to die.

I was absolutely amazed and thrilled. They had become actors! However, the "rooster" didn't know much about crowing, and he sent the audience into fits of laughter. Kris was "Peter," and when Jesus looked at him after the rooster crowed, he went out and "wept bitterly." He wept so convincingly that I could not keep from crying myself. When they nailed "Jesus" to the cross, they made it look very real. The body of "Jesus" convulsed as they hammered the nails, and I wanted to yell "Stop!" I was so proud of them and learned a good lesson. They could do it much better without my involvement.

Christmas was a church holiday. If we missionaries wanted to have a meal together, we had to do it another day other than Christmas. Church activities started early that morning and lasted into the night. Normally, the Citak language congregation merged with the Indonesian language congregation for joint services. December was the hottest season of the year, and snow, cold weather, shopping, Santa Claus, Christmas gifts, and all the other things we connect with Christmas in the U.S., were forgotten. I loved Christmas with the Citak people.

Chapter 26

VAKABUIS

I will not spend much time here telling about the most exciting experience of my life as a missionary, since I have written a book about it titled, *"From Cannibalism to Christianity."*

I had been on the field for about 16 years when we learned about some people who were living deep in the jungle north of Senggo. We wanted to find out who those people were and if they were speaking a dialect of Citak. There were three of those villages: Vakabuis, Bubis, and Esaun.

Being the linguist, it was my awesome privilege to go in on the first very exciting trip to contact the people of Vakabuis. The only way in was by helicopter. There was nowhere for it to land, so the pilot hovered above the logs on the ground while we swung out of the helicopter into the waiting arms of naked cannibals.

The three of us going in on that first trip were Noak Fiak, Dominggus Mayor, and me. You have already read about Noak and Dominggus. I trust that you will read about this in the book, or watch the DVD by the same name.

Now, to the reason for all that has gone before. Analyzing and learning the Citak language, studying their culture, teaching literacy, teaching the people, and winning converts were all leading up to translating the New

Testament into their language. In fact, that was all happening simultaneously.

Chapter 27

BIBLE TRANSLATION

The Citak language has a very fascinating and extremely complicated verbal system. Included in the verb are the tense, mode, time of day, subject, object, benefactive, habitual indicator, durative indicator, indirect relating suffix, causative, etc. For most of you, that probably sounds very confusing. It did to me as well! The verb usually has the main verb, a direction or position indicating auxiliary, and from one to four causatives. As one could imagine, the verbs are very long.

For example:

nandapauapauatikimatupmutmebesna

Translation–"They nailed Him to the cross."

What have you read today? I am sure that most of you have read, at least, a newspaper, or a magazine or a book, in addition to your Bible. Imagine what it would be like if you had nothing to read in English, and if you had never even seen or read any of the Bible in English, or if you had never read any book of any kind.

One of the joys of translating the New Testament and teaching the Citak people was seeing the Bible stories through the eyes of people who had never before heard them. When we were working on translation, I was usually engrossed in how the passage would be translated, while many times, Titus was thinking more about the story. Once, when we were working on a difficult passage written by Paul, Titus said, "Well, Paulus."

I had the impression that he thought that Paul could have said it a way that would have been easier to understand. Often I tended to agree with him.

We were translating the end of one of the gospels and were working on the resurrection of Jesus. As usual, I was thinking about how to translate it, while Titus was more interested in what was happening. Mary had come to the tomb and had run to tell the disciples. Then, she returned to weep at the tomb, and when Jesus appeared and spoke to her, she thought he was the gardener. Titus had been listening intently to the narrative and then said, "Well, Mary, if you just had stayed put, you would have known He had risen."

MAN – STRONG MAN

After the initial translation, we would have a consultant come to Senggo to check it out. This was a requirement by the publisher, and could be very intimidating, especially when the Citak people failed to understand the translation. We would have two or three Citak people whom we called "naïve informants," meaning that they had not helped with the translation and were not familiar with the passage being checked. The consultant did not understand the Citak language, so he would have me read a passage and then have me ask questions of the informants. Hopefully, they would have understood the translation and be able to answer the questions easily. The Citak people could not see something about the translation that was not right and simply say that they either did not understand it or else tell me what was wrong. They would just sit with a confused look on their face and say nothing, much to my embarrassment.

We were working on Mark 3:27–"*No man can enter into a strong man's house, and spoil his goods, except he will first bind the strong man; and then he will spoil his house.*" Narrative is relatively easy to translate, and I expected no problem with their understanding it.

However, much to my chagrin, when I read the passage the informants just sat with very confused looks on their faces. I was embarrassed and thought, "What is their problem? That was an easy passage to translate and I can't figure out what could possibly be wrong with it?" I was not allowed to coach them, so they continued to sit and say nothing.

Finally one of them asked, "How many men were there?"

I answered, "Two men," and reread the passage.

After a long time of trying desperately to figure out what was wrong, one of the men said, "Nona, a 'man' cannot tie up a 'strong man.'" Of course! The man doing the tying must be stronger than the 'strong' man. So sometimes the translation is correct, but doesn't make sense to them. In the other gospels, it makes it clear that the man doing the tying was stronger than the one being tied.

On another occasion, we were checking Matthew 22:23-28, where the Sadducees were asking Jesus about the resurrection. When the first brother died and his brother married the widow, the informants began to laugh. When the same woman married the third brother, they were laughing even more. By the time we had gotten through all seven brothers, they were laughing hysterically. Abdon remarked, "Our women could never do that, they would never live long enough."

This did not happen with us, but I heard of a group in Papua New Guinea who, when asked why Herodias wanted the head of John the Baptist on a platter, understandably answered, "To eat it, of course." We adjusted things so the Citak people would know that she merely wanted John dead, and had no intentions of eating his head.

Mark 2:21, which deals with sewing a new piece of cloth onto an old garment, is a simple verse to translate, but poses a real problem when trying to explain its meaning, Most Citakkers would be thrilled to have a nice new piece of cloth with which to patch their worn out pants.

A SNAKE FOR A FISH? OF COURSE

We were checking Luke 11:11 *"If a son shall ask bread of any of you that is a father, will he give him a stone?"*

The informants answered, "Of course not."

We continued with, *"Or if he ask a fish, will he for a fish give him a serpent?"*

"Yes, of course," they replied.

The Citak people love to eat snake and a good-sized python has much more meat on it than the average fish, so who wouldn't want a snake instead of a fish? When we used a word that meant that it was a poisonous snake and not an average snake, they understood that no good father would give his son a poisonous snake when he asked for a fish.

FAST – PARTY ALL NIGHT

A simple word like a "fast" presents problems. The Citak people will abstain from food as a symbol that someone has died, or that he has been "hit" by an evil spirit. Also, if we translate "fast" as "not to eat," it would probably be understood that there was no food in the house, or that the person was sick. To go without food as a religious observance sounded strange to them.

They had observed our Muslim friends at Senggo during their fast. They saw them have a nightly feast after sundown. However, they had failed to understand that they had gone all day without food. When we came to a passage with "fast" in it, I asked Titus if he knew what it was. He answered, "Yes, it means to party all night." Some explanation was necessary.

In Citak, any second hand information must be indicated by putting the suffix "na" at the end of the utterance. For example, if Gail told me to explain to someone how to take their medicine, I would put the suffix at the end of each sentence and they would know that I was repeating what I had heard Gail say.

When I translated, I had to know whether the writer actually saw or experienced personally what they were writing or if they had heard it directly from someone else. Usually that was not too difficult, but did John actually witness the trial of Jesus, or Peter's denial? Did he actually hear Jesus' prayer in Gethsemane? He was asleep, wasn't he? It was important to use that correctly. For example, if I put it in the first part of Matthew before Jesus called him, the people would be confused and ask, "How did Matthew know those things when he didn't meet Jesus until later?"

WHEN DID THE ROOSTER CROW?

Many people think that translating involves merely taking words and putting them into another language, but it isn't nearly that simple. For example, in Citak every verb must indicate the time of day that the action took place – morning (daylight until about 10:00 a.m.), noon (about 10 a.m. until about 3 p.m.), afternoon (about 3 p.m. until dark), or night (dark until daylight). So, when did the rooster crow?

If I were to ask an American when the rooster crows, they would most likely say that he crows at daybreak. If I were to ask a Citakker the same question he most likely would answer that they usually crow around midnight, but can crow anytime from midnight until after daybreak, and they would be right. We had strange roosters there. So, did the rooster crow at night or in the morning?

We have a hint in Luke 22:66, where Jesus was taken before the council, "as soon as it was day." Since the rooster had already crowed we can conclude that it was still dark. So our problem is solved. Or, is it? In Luke 22:34, Jesus had predicted that Peter would deny him, saying, "...the cock shall not crow this _day_, before that thou shalt thrice deny that thou knowest me." It was already night when Jesus said that, so it would appear that the rooster would have had to crow before midnight or else it was already after midnight when he said it.

However, we must be careful not to try to figure it out from our own English-speaking culture. The Jews counted their days from sundown to sundown. Fortunately for us, the Citak people do the same.

When the doctor asks one of the Citak paramedics to translate for a patient, telling him to take his medicine morning, noon, evening and night, the paramedic will translate it thus, "Take this night, morning, noon and evening." We can conclude, then, that the rooster crowed sometime between the time Jesus predicted it and daylight. So, we had to go through all of that just to know to translate "crow" with the night time-of-day indicator.

WHO IS THE YOUNGER SISTER?

There is no word for "sister" or "brother" in Citak. There are words that mean "younger sister/brother" or "older sister/brother." So, with Mary, Martha, and

Lazarus, for example, I had to know in what order they were born. That presented a few challenges.

APPLYING SCRIPTURE – CITAK STYLE

Translating the Scriptures did have its drawbacks, at times. It was amazing how they could miss so much, and yet could find just one passage that they could use to shame the missionaries.

A favorite verse that I believe they all had memorized was Matthew 5:42 *"Give to him that asketh thee, and from him that would borrow of thee, turn not thou away."*

Another verse that they were fond of quoting was James 2:16. *"And one of you say unto them, depart in peace, be ye warmed and filled; notwithstanding ye give them not those things which are needful to the body; what doth it profit?"* If only we could just teach them to apply other verses as well as they could those.

DEDICATION OF THE FIRST BOOK OF THE NEW TESTAMENT

It was Easter Sunday of 1979. We distributed mimeographed copies of the first book of the Bible in Citak – the book of Mark – and had a special dedication service for it. It was a special day for all of us as Titus distributed the books, and Piet Bakasu gave a message on the importance of the Word of God. Then Titus preached on the resurrection from the book of Mark. Titus read the story very haltingly as the people sat silently, amazed that their language could be written and put into a book.

How thrilling it was in those early days to sit in the services and hear the leader read verses from God's Word, albeit haltingly as he was just learning to read.

It was exciting, too, to hear children memorizing and quoting verses that they were hearing for the first time.

FIRST DRAFT OF CITAK NEW TESTAMENT COMPLETE

The first draft of the Citak New Testament was completed on October 13, 1993. Final checking was finished on August 2, 1994. The consultant was there for about 5 ½ weeks and we worked very hard every day. The presence and help of the Lord was evident in many ways. The Citak helpers were 100% faithful in attendance and worked well. The weather was cooler than I have ever known it to be at Senggo and I survived all the cooking.

One day I was complaining about cooking and Timo said, "Nona, it is a good thing you aren't married. Your husband would beat you every day because you wouldn't want to cook his meals." How true!

CITAK NEW TESTAMENT APPROVED FOR PUBLICATION

Following is an excerpt from my prayer letter in September 1994.

"Thank you for praying about the final checking. We all sensed the presence of the Holy Spirit during this. It has now been approved for publication, and we are doing the final proofreading and manuscript preparation. I cannot express how it feels to be this close to completing this project that has taken so many years, but I realize more and more how incapable I am, and how dependent we are on the Lord to guide us as we finish it, and present it to the publisher. We want to do nothing less than our best."

The goal was to have the translation ready for the printer by December 31, 1994. A missionary colleague, Ted Heglund, formatted the New Testament for us, which we did in Toccoa, Ga. The final touches were made about 2:30 p.m. on December 16th. It was an exciting and memorable time as he handed me the final, formatted copy, all wrapped and ready for me to present to the Indonesian Bible Society to be printed.

Ted Heglund presenting me with the
formatted copy of the Citak N.T.

I guarded it very carefully, like the treasure it was, as I hand carried the precious cargo back to Indonesia and presented it to the Indonesian Bible Society to be published. Then came the difficult waiting period for the printed copies to arrive at Senggo, and for the dedication service.

Chapter 28

GOD SPEAKS CITAK

W e could hardly wait for the first copies of the N.T. to arrive! Finally, the airplane landed with several boxes and I was so excited. I wanted to rip the boxes open immediately right there on the airstrip, but felt that Titus and the others who had worked so hard with me to achieve this milestone should be there for the "unveiling." They were out of the village at the time. I sure got a lesson in patience.

First copies of the Citak N.T. arrive at Senggo

I placed the boxes inside my house and kept looking at them, wanting so badly to open them and to look at the New Testaments. However, with great discipline I resisted the temptation to take even a peep until Titus and the others returned. After they returned and we met at my home, where I even managed to sit aside and allow them to actually open the boxes. What a thrill it was to see the printed Citak New Testament for the first time!

We then hid the books and did not allow anyone else to see them as we waited for the big day when we would have the official dedication service.

The time had finally arrived. It was July – the rainy season. Pilots do not normally fly when it is raining. Visitors from the U.S. were coming and needed to fly all the way across the island from the north coast of Sentani to Senggo.

A LESSON IN PRAYER

I had always had a problem with some of the verses in the Bible that told us to "pray without ceasing," "ask and keep on asking," etc. I did not like the idea of "begging" for anything. I may ask someone for something, but if they don't do it, I will most likely not ask again, but rather will find a way to do it for myself. Besides, doesn't God already know what I need or want? Why should I have to even ask for it to begin with? Furthermore, asking for the same thing over and over from God, Who already knows my request, just did not appeal to me.

In a letter to the folks in the U.S. who were coming out for the dedication service I wrote, "SEE YOU SOON – IF I HAVEN'T PASSED AWAY FROM BEING TOO EXCITED!"

It was the day before the dedication service. A group of friends and family had already arrived in Sentani. Everything was ready at Senggo and I was beside myself with excitement. It was raining. . . and raining. . . and raining, and it seemed that it was never going to stop. The people just had to fly to Senggo the next morning. I began to pray. At first I prayed, "God, I know that You control the rain so I am asking that You stop it." It kept raining. Then I prayed, "Lord, I am trusting You to stop the rain." Oh yeah?

My house had an aluminum roof on it, so there was no mistaking the fact that the rain continued to come down. All night I prayed: "Lord, PLEASE stop the rain. . . Lord, PLEASE stop the rain. . . PLEASE, PLEASE stop the rain. . . Lord, don't you hear that rain? It is still coming down. PLEASE stop the rain."

About 5 a.m. I prayed, "Lord, it is time for the pilot to go out to do the pre-flight check on the airplane, and it is still raining. PLEASE, PLEASE stop the rain."

At about 6 a.m. I further entreated, "Lord, it is time for the pilot to call us and ask for a weather report and it is still raining. PLEASE, PLEASE, PLEASE stop the rain." I had no problem begging God for what He already knew. I learned that begging comes natural when the burden is great.

I can imagine the Holy Spirit presenting my prayers to God something like this, "Father, she is asking that You stop the rain, but that is not really what she wants. She wants her friends to get to Senggo safely for the dedication service. Let's just give her what she really wants, not what she is asking for."

Although the rain did not stop, the courageous pilot came right in there, and landed in the rain with a plane load of people who did not understand the situation enough to be afraid. Five airplanes came in to our small village that day and not one flight was canceled due to the bad weather.

DEDICATION OF THE CITAK NEW TESTAMENT – JULY 16, 1995

The dedication service was attended by about 700 people, 50 of whom were Westerners (Americans), including my brother and sister-in-law, Stan and Jane Stringer, and their daughter, Tamah; the General Director of the mission with his wife, Dr. Richard and Marj Winchell; a supporting pastor and his wife, Rev. and Mrs. Gene Turner; Rhoda Redmond; missionaries from other parts of the island; and, of course, the pilots, as well as some of their families.

Also in attendance were government dignitaries, including the Head of the Police, the Head of the Military, the Head of the civil government, and the District Head, who was the highest ranking civil government leader for the district, and would normally only attend very important programs. Thus, we were honored to have him in attendance. Since the church was too small for the huge crowd, the people built a shelter onto the front of the church to accommodate all the attendees.

We had a banner across the front of the church with the theme, written in both Citak and Indonesian, *"But be ye doers of the Word, and not hearers only..."* James 1:22

In true Indonesian fashion, there were many speeches by the government leaders. The Citak children sang, *"This Little Light of Mine"* and *"The B-I-B-L-E,"* which I had translated into Citak. Copies of the New Testament were presented to the government officials and guests. Titus preached a short message in Citak to the village people.

The Citak people did not often have rice to eat, and whenever we had joint services with the Indonesian congregation, the Citak people always complained that they did not get enough. I wanted this to be the biggest event that Senggo had ever had, and it was. I was determined that no one would be able to complain about not having enough to eat.

The women lined up in the church yard where they built fires on the ground and cooked rice all day in small pots. The men built make-shift tables, and the women laid banana leaves on them for table cloths where they dumped their pots of rice. In total, they cooked 1300 lbs. of rice and four pigs!

Cooking rice

Because of the Indonesian government leaders who were there, it was necessary for the main dedication service to be done in the Indonesian language. However, because we wanted something special just for the Citak people in their own language, on Monday evening we had an informal praise and worship service just for them. At that service, they came to the front of the church, picked up their copy of the N.T. and returned proudly to their seats. That was the service that I enjoyed the most, watching the Citak people holding their New Testaments in their own language for the very first time.

Perhaps the one accomplishment during my time in Papua that causes me to feel the most unworthy yet at the same time so very fulfilled, was the awesome privilege of translating the New Testament into the Citak language. It never would have been accomplished without the help of the Citak people, and without the support of my fellow missionaries at Senggo.

The people of Papua are pretty much isolated from each other due to high mountains and swamps. Because of that, isolation they speak some 700 languages, most of which remain unwritten.

I will never forget one day when a man from the neighboring Auyu tribe came to my house requesting a Bible. I asked him, "Do you want it in Indonesian?"

"No, I want it in Auyu," he answered.

"There is no Auyu Bible," I told him.

He asked, "Would you order one for me?"

It broke my heart to have to say, "There is no Auyu Bible, because it has never been translated."

On another occasion, a group of men came from the village of Saman, which belonged to the neighboring Asmat tribe. They "voted" in their village and sent those men as their representatives to inform me that they had decided that I would move to Saman and translate the New Testament into their language. It saddened me to have to tell them that I could not do it.

The village of Tamnim, which I have already mentioned, was located just a few minutes from my house. The people of that village spoke another language, a dialect of Asmat, which was different from the one spoken at Saman. I had already translated a song book, selected verses, and a Bible study course in their language. After the dedication of the Citak New Testament they came to me asking, "When do we get our New Testament?"

Chapter 29

GOD SPEAKS TAMNIM

After the dedication of the Citak New Testament we began working on the translation of the Asmat dialect of Tamnim. Although the Citak-speaking people and the Tamnim people could not understand each other, there were many similarities between the two languages. Therefore, the Tamnim project moved much faster, since it was not actually a translation, as such, but rather a dialect adaptation. Even so, it took five years to complete.

By now we had computers, which were powered by a 12-volt auto battery. We had electricity for about four hours at night, when the battery was recharged. All my work was done on the computer and without it my work would have come to a halt. One day the computer died. Usually, the soonest that something like that can be repaired is at least a month. I would have to send it out on the next flight from Senggo to a man on the north coast in Sentani who might get around to it quickly, but most likely would not.

Since I could not work anyway, I decided that rather than send it out to be repaired I would take it myself in order to expedite the work. It just happened that we had a flight going out the very next day, and I was determined that I would be on it.

We were all amazed about how the Lord put people in just the right place. I arrived in Sentani on Tuesday afternoon, only to discover that the part I needed could only be found in the Indonesian capital of Jakarta. I would have to have someone in Jakarta purchase it for me, and then find a way to get it back to our island. That in itself could take weeks.

Our pilot, Bob Breuker, was in Jakarta at the time, and went right out and purchased the part. It just so happened that another pilot, John Miller, was returning to Papua from furlough that very night and would be coming through Jakarta.

Bob took the part to the airport, negotiated his way into the waiting room, and gave the part to John, who brought it to Sentani. The computer expert in Sentani put the part in my computer in about ten minutes. I have no doubt whatsoever that God was working on behalf of the Tamnim people.

WOMEN SHOULD KEEP QUIET IN CHURCH

Gerson Arenu and Hendruk Emenu were working with me. One day we were working on translating the passage in which Paul wrote that women should keep quiet in church, and if they had any questions they should ask their husbands at home. I said kiddingly, "Since I don't have a husband, can I talk in church?" Hendruk, not realizing that I was joking, looked very serious and sympathetic and said, "Yes, Nona, *you* can talk in church." I told him that I would tell Paul that I had permission!

In 2000, after completing the Tamnim translation, we held another dedication service.

At the dedication service, they again came up to the front of the church to pick up their New Testaments. I will never forget Wapet, the old village chief. He cannot read a thing, but he proudly picked up his New Testament, and returned to his seat, hugging his precious New Testament to his chest.

I wish I had another life where I could translate more of God's Word for the precious people in Papua.

Hendruk and Gerson

Chapter 30

HOW DO YOU SAY GOODBYE?

H ave you been wondering if I have forgotten about the little boys in the red shorts about whom I wrote in Chapter 2? Well, I did not forget.

After I arrived at Senggo, and had begun to learn the Citak language, one day I told the men with whom I was working about those little boys whom God had used to point me to Papua. They looked at each other and with big smiles exclaimed, "Those little boys were us."

They were Titus, Noak, and Abdon, as well as others who were the first leaders in the Citak church and who worked with me in translating the Citak New Testament. God used a picture of those little boys to speak to a young lady in Bible school, and then many years later brought us all together in the village of Senggo. What an amazing God we serve!

Before I left for the field, the mission board did all they could to prepare me for what I was about to do. I was 24 years old, very naïve, and had not ever been on an airplane. The mission board told us that once we got on the airplane and left the U.S., nothing would ever be the same again. Someone would no doubt die before we came home again. Family members would grow up and change. Friends would go on with their lives and the friendships we enjoyed would never be like they were before. We were encouraged to immerse ourselves into the language, lives, and culture of the people where we were going. They tried to prepare us to go but failed to prepare us to return!

The time was approaching for me to return to the U.S. to retire for good. It was a scary thought! A short time before I was to leave the field, a man died in the village of Senggo. I spent most of the day with the mourners and had gone with them into the jungle to bury the corpse.

While the men were filling in the grave I went over and sat down on a log to wait. I was sitting there wearing culottes, a tank top and flip flops. I was very dirty from being with the ladies who had been rolling in the mud as a sign of mourning. I was also very hot and sweaty, and mosquitoes were buzzing around me, and bugs were crawling up my legs. I thought, "I am at home. I am comfortable. I know what is expected of me and I know what to do."

I knew that when I came home I would feel intimidated, and would not know what was expected of me. I would not know what people were talking about when they discussed current news and politics. I would not really know my own family members because I had been out of their lives for 40 years. They would not be able to understand where I had come from, and what it had meant to me to leave "my people." In some ways, the idea of returning was scarier than when I first went to the field.

The Citak people had become my family and I had grown to love them very much. I loved it when they called me "Mama" and "Grandma." I knew them and they knew me. The entire Senggo community held a "Going Away Reception," which was attended by the Citak, Tamnim, and Indonesian language congregations, as well as many others, including our Catholic and Muslim friends, along with government representatives.

There were many hugs and lots of tears as the time approached for the airplane to come for my final departure. The people congregated at the airstrip, and mourned as they showed their love for me. At that time, I expected that I would never be able to return. As I boarded the airplane I looked at them, and thought that it would be the last time I would ever see them this side of Heaven. I felt that everyone I knew had died all at the same time.

I am weeping as I write this as I reminisce about the 40 years I was allowed the privilege of serving the Lord in Papua. As I remember a very naïve 12 year-old girl who "just knew" that God had called me to be a missionary, how He marvelously led me to get me there, and His amazing grace that kept me there, all I can say is: "Jesus led me all the way."

9 781498 403030